MW01128231

Disaster Prep for The Rest of Us

or

What to Do When the Lights Go Out

Dave Robinson

Copyright © 2014 Dave Robinson

ISBN 978-1-63263-927-1

Library of Congress Cataloguing in Publication Data
Robinson, David N.
Disaster Prep for the Rest of Us by Dave Robinson
Reference / Survival & Emergency Preparedness
Library of Congress Control Number: 2014944891

Published by BookLocker.com, Inc., Bradenton, Florida.

Printed in the United States of America.

Abuzz Press
2014

First Edition

DISCLAIMER

This book details the author's personal experiences with and opinions about Disaster Preparedness.

The author and publisher are providing this book and its contents on an "as is" basis and make no representations or warranties of any kind with respect to this book or its contents. The author and publisher disclaim all such representations and warranties, including for example warranties of merchantability and advice for a particular purpose. In addition, the author and publisher do not represent or warrant that the information accessible via this book is accurate, complete or current.

The statements made about products and services have not been evaluated by the U.S. government. Please consult with your own legal or accounting professional regarding the suggestions and recommendations made in this book.

Except as specifically stated in this book, neither the author or publisher, nor any authors, contributors, or other representatives will be liable for damages arising out of or in connection with the use of this book. This is a comprehensive limitation of liability that applies to all damages of any kind, including (without limitation) compensatory; direct, indirect or consequential damages; loss of data, income or profit; loss of or damage to property and claims of third parties.

You understand that this book is not intended as a substitute for consultation with a licensed medical, legal or accounting professional. Before you begin any change your lifestyle in any way, you will consult a licensed professional to ensure that you are doing what's best for your situation.

This book provides content related to Disaster Preparedness topics. As such, use of this book implies your acceptance of this disclaimer.

Table of Contents

Introduction

Ok, admit it. You promise yourself every year that you're going to put together a few extra supplies, just in case. Everybody from the Red Cross to the government, to the local newspaper suggests that you "Get A Kit, Make A Plan, and Be Prepared." And every year, you mean to, you really do. And the next thing you know, there's an earthquake off in some faraway place or a hurricane on the other end of the country and you think, "I've really *got* to do this thing!"

But where to start? What to do first? Which kit to buy? What will my friends think? Here's my approach, "Just pretend that the power goes out all over the area, and you can't get to the store for at least three days. What are you going to need to get by?"

Some time back, a fast-moving storm decimated the region from Ohio eastward. One survivor made the following observation: "On the first day, all the hardware stores were stripped of generators by 9:00 AM and by noon, almost all of the gas canisters at most stores were sold out leaving people to form lines at gas stations in the squelching heat. By 4:00 PM the grocery stores were stripped of food, water and other essentials, such as ice. Within a day, everything was gone." He went on to say that, "Water is so much more important than most realize, I highly recommend people stock up on storable water and water filters. A portable burner is a must. You will need some sort of power to heat your food, especially since most food, even storable food requires water and is best eaten when heated."

So in the event of a disaster and depending on your priorities, you're going to need to eat, cook, and find your way around in the dark. And that's just for starters. So here's what you do...Haul out that old camping stove and see if it still works. Clean it up, put some fresh fuel in it and fire it up. While you're at it, dig out your lantern and do the same with it. They may just come in handy. If you don't own either and you are solely dependent on electricity for all your energy needs, then you need to pick up at least a stove. (Watch garage sales for some real bargains.) Now make sure you have fresh batteries for your flashlight. There are lots of battery-powered lanterns on the market.

Now, see how easy that was, and you're on your way to getting your kit together. And oh, by the way, I don't suggest that folks buy a kit. There are hundreds on the market, they usually have stuff in them that you will never use, items that don't fit your needs, and some kits even have (gasp!) low quality components. It is always best to assemble your own kit. That way you will know what you have and exactly what you don't have. Besides you can go online and see what the commercially available kits have in them, and get ideas for your own. Just remember, survival is not a kit anyway, but it does help to have a few things together. Skills and information are more important than stuff.

Disaster preparedness doesn't have to break your budget, but with a little careful planning, you can, over time, accumulate a few things that will make life a whole lot easier the next time the lights go out.

Mindsets

There are those who make things happen, those who watch what happens and those who wonder what happened. I find a similar set of breakdowns when it comes to disaster preparedness.

The first group is absolutely convinced the sky will fall in at any moment. Society will collapse, electrical power will be cut off, and gangs of lawless marauders will be running free in the streets. But this group has it covered, they have planned ahead. Their "bug out location" is hidden in the mountains, well fortified and stocked with beans, bullets and band aids. Their "bug out vehicle" is fully capable of carrying all their bug out gear and is ready to spirit them and their family to safety. These people are gung-ho and fully committed to their cause. For them, disaster preparedness is almost a form of religion to be preached and practiced to a level of high fanaticism

At the other end of the spectrum is the guy who, for whatever reason, has no intention of making any kind of preparations. When the topic comes up in conversation his response goes something like this: "Well if anything happens, I'll just come to your house." That's the best way I know to irritate a prepper. To which one person replied, "Why would you take food out of the mouths of my children when you had ample warning to prepare?"

No matter where a person finds themselves in this discussion, sooner or later you may be required to rely on what you have set aside. Your disaster may be nothing more than a wind storm that takes down the power lines between you and the grocery store, or it could be a 9.0 mega quake that devastates an entire region for weeks. Either way you will fare better with just a bit of foresight, a few of the basics on your shelves and an attitude that says, "We'll get through this, and hopefully help out our neighbors along the way."

Most of us, I'm sure, fall somewhere in the middle of the debate. Not quite fanatical, but not quite complacent either. So now is the time to get started. On your next trip to the grocery store, watch for sales; pick up some non-perishable foods strictly for the purpose of setting them aside. Next time, do the same. Search your closets and drawers for old candles. You know, the ones that are either broken or just don't match your decor this month. Presto, emergency lighting.

We're Not Ready!

Did you ever wonder how many folks are really making preparations for a disaster? How many are actually stocking up on extra groceries or even considering their need to make plans to survive a catastrophic event? A recent national poll by Adelphi University Center for Health Innovation surveyed 1,000 Americans about their personal preparedness behaviors and the results show that we're not ready!

More than half of Americans have not prepared copies of their vital documents. Things like the title deed to your house, insurance policies, social security cards and any other document you think is important, should be copied and stored in a safe place outside your own home. That way if your house burns in a wildfire or is somehow destroyed, you at least have proof you own it. Scanning to a flash drive or to an online cloud application is another method of saving documents. (If you don't do computers, then refer to the first sentence about making copies and the safe place plan.) Getting your life back to normal after a disaster will be easier if you can prove who you are, what you own, when you were born or even whether or not you are a legal citizen.

48% of those surveyed lacked emergency supplies for use in the event of an emergency. Frankly I'm surprised the number isn't higher. But considering most people have roughly a two week supply of food in the house anyway, it's the other essentials they're short on. Things like flashlights, batteries, battery powered radio or water. After the disaster strikes is not a good time to head for the store. Stores may be closed (or sold out), roads may be impassable and ATMs won't work anyway, so stock up before you need to. Trying to stock up after the event is a bit like trying to buy insurance after you've had the fender bender.

More than half of parents surveyed do not have a designated meeting place in case of disaster. During the 2010 Haiti earthquake, hundreds of children were separated from families. The American Red Cross offers a service called "Safe and Well". "Safe and Well" helps reconnect loved ones after an emergency. Check it out at their website: www.redcross.org. The conversation with your family should establish two meeting places, one directly outside your house in case of fire, and one outside your neighborhood in case you can't get home right away.

August 1, 2007, a bridge collapsed in Minneapolis, Minnesota, right during afternoon rush hour. Thirteen people were killed, hundreds injured and traffic snarled for miles in all direction. Thousands of folks were calling families and loved ones to report in. Many calls were never completed as the demand on the cell phone system overloaded the circuits and generated frustration and concern all over the city. What some learned was that text messages were far more likely to go through than were voice messages. So take a hint from that experience; if you are ever in the middle of a disaster, text home. If you don't know how to text, ask any kid. They love to show us grown-ups how to work our electronics.

It all starts with extra flashlight batteries, or a new camp stove, or buy one, get one at the grocery store. Or maybe something as simple (and potentially lifesaving) as designating a meeting place if you wake up at night and smell smoke.

The Fear Factor

I always wear my seat belt. I wear a helmet when I ride a motorcycle. Most of us have learned, and are convinced; these things are in our best interest, just in case something goes wrong. I do these things because in the event of an accident I am protected. I do not wear them out of fear, but out of wisdom. An ancient Hebrew proverb says, "A wise man foresees trouble and plans for it. A fool goes on blindly and suffers the consequences."

If you make preparations out of fear, then you're going to a lot of effort for the wrong reasons. Several months back we held a Disaster Preparedness class at our church. About 25 people attended. At the class we discussed being prepared, having a kit, making a plan and being informed. Among the topics discussed was the probability of an earthquake off the coast followed by a tsunami and the impact such an event would have on our region. One of the attendees was a young mom who went home, grabbed her kids and pitched a tent out in a field near her house for fear of an earthquake leveling her home in the night. That's not exactly what we had in mind when we scheduled the class.

The point is, get your kit together but not out of fear. Make your plans and preparations out of wisdom so that when things do go wrong you will be better off than others. You will be in a position to extend help to your neighbors rather than being a victim. We have spare tires in our vehicles, not because we're afraid of having a flat, but "just in case." I carry Band-Aids in my wallet, "just in case." We don't make preparations out of fear, but just in case.

I recently read an article in our local newspaper headlined, "Deputies rescue two motorists stuck in snow." It seems that this couple (Mensa candidates, I'm sure) was on a Forest Service road somewhere in Central Oregon, when they became stuck in the snow. After trying to get unstuck, the guy takes off on foot for help. Eventually the woman gets worried and dials 911. He gets very cold after walking about three miles, turns around and goes back to the vehicle. The story has a happy ending as searchers find them in their vehicle that same evening. Now get this, a Deputy Sheriff reports that the man was wearing tennis shoes, jeans and a T-shirt. Huh?

Okay, let's analyze this. Number one, if they have cell service why didn't they just call for help to begin with? And secondly, a T-shirt?! Are you kidding me? Don't you think that if you are going to be out in the hills playing in the snow you might at least have a sweatshirt or jacket? After all you *could* get stuck and have to walk out. Lady Luck was truly with them as not many of the canyons and gullies in our area have cell phone coverage. At least he did have the presence of mind to get back to the vehicle, but overall I'd give him a "D" minus in survival sense.

The REAL First Responders

"They" are always there. Pick up your phone in any emergency, dial 9-1-1 and you get a response. They are the first ones on the scene. That's why they're called "First Responders." Whether it's the Fire Department, Police, Sheriff's Deputies, State Police or Ambulance (EMS) personnel, we have learned to rely on their dedication, professionalism and faithful attendance to our emergency needs.

But what if, just what if you dial that number and nobody responds? In the event of a disaster, "they" are going to have their hands full and your emergency is going to take a low priority. If you can get through at all. That's why your neighbors are your REAL first responders. All across the country neighborhoods are forming N.E.P.P. groups (Neighborhood Emergency Preparedness Plan). Using a technique known as "mapping your neighborhood," neighborhoods are getting organized, inventorying their skills, equipment and their demographics.

In my opinion, this is the **single most important thing** you can do to be prepared against disaster. Any disaster. Organizing your neighborhood. This is not another government-sponsored program. This is a grass-roots, community based effort designed to bring people together. For example are there seniors in your neighborhood who will need assistance in the event of a disaster? Which of your neighbors has infants, toddlers or possibly special needs children? Who has plumbing or electrical skills? Which of your neighbors has medical skills? Who can run a chain saw (everyone in Oregon) or who has access to a backhoe? Mapping your neighborhood documents all of this. Which of your neighbors has natural gas that may need to be shut off in the event of an earthquake? Where are the propane tanks located? Which ones are handicapped? Is anyone insulin-dependent? Their insulin will need to be refrigerated. Anyone on oxygen? Mapping your neighborhood will create an inventory of all these matters and will save lives in the event of a disaster.

The need is for people to get involved. If you've ever wanted to do something of significance for your community short of running for public office, here's your chance. This will require someone in each neighborhood contacting your neighbors to bring them together for this endeavor. If this interests you and you'd like more information you can contact the local emergency services coordinator. They will be happy to provide you with the information you need to get started.

Let's play a little game of pretend. A major disaster has hit your neighborhood. The electricity just winked off all over town. Maybe a tornado or earthquake or hurricane-force winds. You're pretty sure there's damage on your neighbor's house so you pick up the phone to call 9-1-1. The line is dead. Cell phone, "Sorry all circuits are busy try your call again later," in that irritating, metallic voice you hate to hear. You can't reach anyone. But you feel a responsibility to your neighbor, after all she's an elderly lady, lives alone and someone should probably go check on her. Not only that a big tree just fell across her house. She could be injured. You try the cell phone again. Same answer. Pick up the landline, still dead.

The reality is that during a major catastrophic event, YOU are the first responder. This is why neighborhoods all across the country are instituting a program called 'Mapping Your Neighborhood'. This is a simple grass-roots plan that relies on people organizing their own neighborhoods and building a network of contacts based on who lives on your block or in your immediate vicinity. Generally made up of fewer than 20 homes, a list is compiled of who lives where. Do they have natural gas or a propane tank? Is there an elderly person in the home, one who may need assistance in the event of a disaster. Are they on oxygen? How about insulin? Does anyone have a toddler or infant in the home? On the other hand, is anyone in your neighborhood equipped with a backhoe, generator, chainsaw or other item that could come in handy during a crisis? How about skills? Is anyone trained in medical care, maybe a nurse or someone who can give care to an elderly person or a young child? Does anyone have carpentry skills? Anyone skilled in counseling, maybe a minister?

All these questions will be answered at your first neighborhood meeting. What is needed is for someone to grasp the vision of seeing their neighborhood come together and get organized on a very local level. Only one meeting per year is really necessary and only then to refresh files and acquaintances. Some groups simply compile a list of their neighbors and make a basic plan while others do fundraisers to buy needed equipment like fire extinguishers or community-owned chainsaws. The extent of involvement is strictly up to the local neighborhood.

To begin simply search online for "Mapping Your Neighborhood Oregon." You will find a booklet you can print off to get you started. If politics isn't exactly your thing, but you want to contribute to your neighborhood, this may be just the opportunity for you. There is no federal funding, but most cities in our region have someone who is designated to assist with disaster preparedness.

Asset or Liability?

Asset or liability? Terms normally reserved for bean counters, accountants and other bookkeeping types. In the event of a disaster there are both. Those who are part of the problem and those who are part of the solution. Assets and liabilities. I have already mentioned the probable lack of ability of our first responders to answer every need in the event a major disaster. Not through any fault of theirs. The first responders I know are dedicated professionals who train ceaselessly and devote their lives to public service. It's simply a matter of being overwhelmed when anything of disastrous significance occurs. It is routinely understood among fire, EMS and law enforcement people that they will be unable to respond to most calls for assistance. In short, they need more assets.

My wife and I spent a recent weekend attending Community Emergency Response Team (C.E.R.T.) training. Along with twenty others we had classes on first-aid, triage, light search and rescue, terrorism and other related topics. The concept of a trained cadre of citizens was developed by the Los Angeles Fire Department in 1985 to augment their staff in time of disaster. Today the program is under the covering of F.E.M.A. and the administration trickles down to the local fire departments through the county's Emergency Services Coordinator. C.E.R.T. volunteers were recently activated during the recent rash of tornadoes in the south and in the Joplin, Missouri, tornado.

On March 11, 2011, when the tsunami from the Japanese earthquake threatened our coast, a dozen C.E.R.T. members from Astoria and neighboring towns were activated. The team reported to a local elementary school to set up a tsunami shelter. They brewed coffee and prepared food for the firefighters who had been up all night trying to warn people to relocate, as well as for citizens who came to weather a possible tsunami wave. C.E.R.T. staged these activities from its "C.E.R.T.mobile" a former ambulance that not only has food-preparation space, but also holds emergency equipment, including chainsaws, generators, floodlights, traffic signs, and radios for all law enforcement and amateur radio channels. The C.E.R.T. coordinators kept in constant contact with amateur radio operators observing conditions along the coast.

The C.E.R.T. members staffed the post until it became clear later that morning that their area would not be hit by the tsunami, although parts of the southern Oregon and northern California coasts were damaged.

It's your call. Asset? Or liability? The training will be offered again in a few months and will benefit anyone who attends. Not only that, but your newfound skills and energy will become an asset to your community. If interested contact your local Department of Emergency Management to get your name on the list for training.

Y.O.Y.O.
(You're On Your Own)

I know I keep mentioning this, but in the event of a major disaster, YOU ARE ON YOUR OWN! Several weeks after Superstorm Sandy came ashore on the other coast people were still without power. Essential services are slow to be restored and government resources are insufficient to "fix it" for everyone.

In spite of all this, I still have people tell me that in lieu of preparing for a disaster, their "plan" is to rely on government services or local charities. This may seem harsh, but in the words of John Wayne, "Life is tough, but it's tougher when you're stupid!" It doesn't take a genius to see that local services are dangerously overwhelmed during any emergency, let alone a storm like Sandy or similar event.

I will concede that F.E.M.A. and other disaster responders have come a long way in the years since Katrina. Supplies are pre-positioned more quickly and resources are in place far more rapidly than in times past. Still, nothing trumps personal preparedness. To have your own stores and plans in place means you have to rely on no one. If you have done your homework, you know what you have at your disposal and are familiar not only with your local geography but with the local weather habits.

Knowing what you have on hand is essential. After the power goes out and blown-down trees are blocking your route to the grocery store is no time to find out what you're lacking. Secondly, knowing your way around is essential. Familiarize yourself with alternate routes. Now would be a good time to purchase a good quality local map showing all the side roads or back roads in your neighborhood. Then after you buy the map, go for a drive some nice afternoon and prove out the accuracy of your map. (Experience talking here!) If you're new to the area, find out which roads flood first. And while you're at it, find out which roads stay frosty and slick all day after the temperatures dip below freezing at night.

Locally speaking, we are very fortunate, weather-wise. Our region gets neither severe winter blizzards, nor the hurricanes of the eastern and gulf states. Our temperatures are moderate and for the most part, the occasional wind storm is manageable. Primarily we have to contend with the odd high-wind and rain storm during the winter months. A major earthquake has been predicted for our coast and when that occurs, it will be a life-changing event. Make no mistake about it. Those folks on the east coast have certainly had their lives changed! Get prepared because Y.O.Y.O!

One of the problems with disasters is they have no soul. They don't discriminate and they don't care who they hurt. As evidenced by the recent monster tornado in Oklahoma, the only advantage you have in some instances, is your level of preparedness.

After a disaster, there are two kinds of people, those who have been injured (or worse) and those who have not. The casualties are out of the game, so to speak, and the rest of us (the uninjured) fall into two categories. There are those who are equipped to handle a disaster and there are those who, for one reason or another, never thought this could happen to them and have failed to prepare.

Of the survivors, there are assets and liabilities. Those who have sought out training or set about storing up supplies have just become assets. The survivors who have neither training nor supplies, are now liabilities. They, in many cases, are a drain on the resources, much like the injured.

The military knows when the shooting starts, soldiers don't necessarily panic, rather they perform to the level of their training. When the bullets start flying, their programming takes over and how they have been trained becomes their pattern of behavior. The more intense the training, the more "routine" the activity seems. Instead of running wildly in a circle, a trained combat soldier will get down, seek cover and concealment and hopefully live to see another day. All because of training.

For those trained in First Aid, coming across a traffic accident is simply another exercise except now the blood is real and so is the pain. These are the ones who become assets in time of disaster. Humans tend to rise to the level of their training in a crisis. Maybe it's time to ask yourself: What am I trained for? When's the last time I was pushed into a crisis? How would I respond in a REAL disaster? Would I be an asset or a liability?

Why not seek out a First Aid class? Even if you don't think you could ever be used in a disaster, maybe you could be the family hero when your charge needs something slightly more than a Band-Aid. At least your training in triage gives you an understanding of what needs to go to the emergency room and what can be treated at home.

Citizen Emergency Response Team (CERT) training is held periodically and is a weekend well-spent that will equip you to be a huge asset to your community in the event of a disaster. In fact many jurisdictions won't even let would-be volunteers into the disaster area without CERT validation. The attitude of the on-scene commanders is that someone without proper credentials is simply one more liability, but a CERT member can help lessen the load of the full-time emergency responders.

So what will it be? Asset or liability? The choice is yours.

C.O.O.P.

Everybody likes to poke fun at the government, especially the post office. I have worked for the Postal Service for over 30 years and have heard all the horror stories, complaints and "suggestions." And yes, I admit, we do make mistakes, but we also do lots of things right. One of the things that we do well is keeping the mail moving when nothing else seems to be.

When Hurricane Katrina simply wiped some post offices off their foundations and filled others with water and debris, the Postal Service was one of the first agencies to respond quickly and kept the mail moving in areas while other government services were paralyzed for days, and in some cases, weeks.

Each year every postmaster is required to complete a Continuation Of Operations Plan (C.O.O.P.). This plan lists the personnel who are capable of providing leadership in an emergency, alternate post office in the area if your local office is somehow rendered unusable, and a plan to keep the mail flowing as much as possible. For those of us on the South Coast of Oregon, keeping the mail moving to and from the region will depend on the bridges remaining in service and the roads being open, which in the event of an earthquake may or may not be realistic. The experts tell us a major quake will isolate us for several weeks due to closed roads and bridges. That will affect the trucks which transport our mail as well. Limited mail service could possibly be handled by airplane or helicopter until the roads are again made passable. While I'm on the topic, your grocer's trucks won't be able to get through either. Experience in other areas has taught us that grocery store shelves empty out within hours of a major event. I'm not here to scare you, but you really do need to be putting aside some groceries.

For those who receive medication by mail, this is another matter to consider. Connecting with your doctor to arrange an extra supply of needed prescriptions would be something you may want to discuss on your next visit.

Back to C.O.O.P., if you own a business, do you have a plan to continue operations without power? If an event happens during mid-workday and your employees can't get home, is your workplace set up to provide for their needs until they can get home? I realize this is taking the conversation to a higher level, but if you're serious about being ready, these are questions you need to ask yourself. This would be a good topic of discussion for your next staff meeting. Asking, and finding answers for, the hard questions now will lessen some of the hard decisions you may have to make when the time comes.

Earthquake! Not If, But When

No conversation about disaster preparedness would be complete without mentioning earthquakes. Historically we in the Northwest are visited by a major offshore seismic event every 300-600 years. There have been many quakes in Oregon in recent history, but the last notable quake to strike our region was in 1700. The general consensus among geologists is that it's not a matter of 'if' it happens again, but rather a matter of 'when'.

Major earthquakes out in the ocean generate tsunamis. Most of us remember the December quake a few years back when the ensuing tsunami struck Southeast Asia, then again the Japanese earthquake on March 11, 2011 followed up by the relentless destruction of a tsunami. So if the experts are right, we can expect a tsunami-generating quake off the coast at any moment.

Communities along the coast are in significant danger depending on the size and location of the quake. Every coastal city in Oregon has taken the matter seriously by installing tsunami warning systems, safe centers and signs pointing to escape routes. Local officials believe this is not a matter to be taken lightly.

Aside from the initial damage, there are two major problems I see when it comes to quakes. First, electrical power will be interrupted for a lengthy period of time, shutting down most banking (including ATM/Debit service) and retail stores. Secondly, roads and bridges will be impassable based on the strength and location of the seismic event. Next time you drive out of the area, count the bridges that will require inspection following a quake before ODOT will allow their use. Also count the 'cuts' in the hillsides that may liquefy and block the road. Not only will we be isolated and restricted from traveling to the outside, but any efforts to be resupplied will be restricted due to impassable roads.

In regards to communications, you can plan on your landline phones to be down for a time. Depending on whether or not the cell phone towers and fiber optic cables remain intact, we may or may not have cell service. While I'm on the topic of cell phones; In the event of any disaster, take a hint from the kids and use your texting function. Sending a text message uses less 'space' on the system and greatly increases the chance of your message getting through. 'Voice' messages will often get a recording, "Sorry all circuits are busy, please try your call again later." Not what you want to hear when trying to connect with your family. If you don't know how to text on your cell phone, just ask the nearest kid.

FEMA and the Red Cross have always advised us to have food and supplies to last 72 hours, no wait, seven days, even better, 14 days. So you get your kit together, and you've got some peace of mind. That winter storm can come and you've got no worries, an earthquake can strike and your chances of survival are greatly increased.

During An Earthquake

Periodically we read of earthquakes off our coast in the 2.5 to 4.0 range. They rarely generate any trouble for us. These are being viewed as either practice for the "Big One" or a stress reliever for the ever-moving tectonic plates. We have previously explored what to do in preparation for an earthquake. In this installment we're going to learn what to do *during* a seismic event. As I've mentioned earlier, most Oregonians are unfamiliar with earthquakes and as a result, we don't know how to behave during a seismic event.

Indoors. The approved technique here is DROP, COVER and HOLD ON. My instinct always told me that if I were inside a building, I should GET OUT! Wrong. More people are killed by falling building debris than being crushed by pancaked buildings. So DROP to the floor so you don't get knocked down by the violent shaking. Get under something solid like a strong table or desk, that's the COVER part. If there's nothing to get under, cover your head and face and HOLD ON until the shaking stops.

Stay away from glass, windows, outside doors and walls and anything that could fall. If you're in bed, stay there. Protect yourself with your pillow unless you are under a heavy light fixture or fan that could fall. In that case move out of harm's way. And don't go jump in the bathtub, that's the wrong disaster. That's for tornadoes.

Doorways are a good refuge if you know they are a good solid, load-bearing doorway, and if they are close by. Don't go running around trying to find a protective doorway. More injuries occur when people are looking for a sheltered spot than if they had just dropped to the floor to ride out the event.

Outdoors. If you're outdoors, stay there. Move away from trees, power lines and anything that could potentially fall on you. Ground movement is seldom the cause of fatalities, rather falling debris from collapsing buildings, shattered, flying glass and other falling objects are the biggest killers.

In a moving vehicle. Stop as soon as possible. Stay in the vehicle. Avoid overpasses, stopping under or beside buildings, bridges, utility wires and trees.

During emergencies we humans perform to our level of training. Whatever we have learned to do in a panic situation will dictate our behavior. Don't take time trying to decide what to do when it happens. Make up your mind right now what you're going to do, and when the shaking starts, *do it!* The anatomy of an earthquake is such that you must act quickly to stay safe. Deal with your normalcy bias and be ready to respond when you feel the first shake. Doing so will provide leadership to those around you; minimize your own chance of injury and quite possibly save the life of someone else.

Tsunami Tsafety

Every city on the Oregon Coast has a tsunami warning system in place. Officials in coastal communities have taken the threat of earthquake/tsunami seriously enough to create evacuation routes and a warning system designed to minimize casualties. Those little signs point the way to higher ground and safety from an incoming tsunami. I'm always mildly amused by the sign that says, "Leaving Tsunami Zone." How do they know? What if that sucker is two feet higher, or ten feet higher than their signpost? Now I'm not privy to all of the scientific planning that went in to marking the zone, but I'm assuming that their data is solid and was attained through sound processes. Just to be on the safe side, if I'm on the way out, running from a tsunami, I'm not stopping at that sign!

Another thing not mentioned on the "evacuation route" signs is that if the anticipated earthquake is as severe as many think it will be, there is no way we can jump in our cars and simply drive our way to high ground. Streets will be broken, bridges impassable, building debris is likely to cover the road, power poles and power lines will block streets and trees are apt to have fallen in inconvenient places. More and more I'm hearing that folks are being instructed to "walk" to higher ground. I'm thinking "run" is more like it, but some of us don't run much anymore. Not for very far anyway.

Also if you're on the beach or at sea level and you feel the shaking of a quake, don't wait for the siren. That shaking is likely the only warning you will get. Computer simulations have demonstrated that on January 26, 1700, when the last Cascadia Subduction Zone earthquake stuck our coast, it is estimated that there was a 20 to 30 minute time period before the initial tsunami wave hit. Geologic history has showed waves were as high as 30 feet.

Another evacuation tactic is also being suggested: vertical evacuation. That is, finding a sturdy building at least three stories high and climbing to at least the third story.

Two important keys here: STURDY building and THREE stories high!

Earthquake Science 101

By now everyone knows that earthquakes are caused by a rumbling deep inside the earth and if the rumbling is severe enough, there is damage here on the surface. The amount of damage depends on several factors including the type of quake, and location. Most folks look for a measure of intensity from the newsperson; "There was a quake last night in Outer Slobovia which measured 6.2 on the Richter Scale." We know that was a quake of moderate strength. The higher the number, the more intense the quake, thus the more danger to life and property..

In 1935 Charles Richter developed a scale based on seismographic readings to measure the intensity of earthquakes. For several decades his scale was the state of the art for earthquake measurement. But technology being what it is, the Richter magnitude scale eventually became obsolete, mostly because of its limitations in accurately measuring the quake several miles from the epicenter. Then one of his peers improved on the original and it became the Modified Richter Scale. Again technology drove the geology community to improve and along came the Mercalli scale.

While the Modified Richter Scale is still used to measure the intensity of the quake, the Mercalli Scale is used to measure the effects of the quake. The effects are varied, compared to the distance from the epicenter. Then to further complicate matters, in the 1970s, along came the Moment Magnitude Scale (MMS). The magnitude is based on the *seismic moment* of the quake. A formula involving the rigidity of the Earth, the amount of slip on the fault, and size of the area that slipped, measures the MMS. Fortunately for the layman, the numbers to report the MMS are the same as the Richter Scale numbers.

I realize all this can be confusing, but hang on. Did you know that an earthquake measuring 3.0 is ten times stronger than one measuring 2.0? We are conditioned to break down numbers in tenths. For example a sign reading 6.5 miles, means 6 and one half miles. Not so with the Richter Scale. Using ordinary logic, you'd think a 6.0 earthquake would be twice as intense as a 3.0. Not so, in reality it is three-hundred percent greater!

Scientists can come pretty close with predicting where quakes will happen, but even with all of today's technology and measuring equipment, it is still impossible to accurately predict when they will strike. Thanks to GPS technology and literally thousands of sensors drilled deep within the earth's crust, plate movement can be recorded as little as one-half centimeter. Even as you read this, the Cascade Mountains are rising and tilting eastward as the Juan de Fuca plate pushes under the Continental Plate along the Cascadia Fault about 60 or so miles off our coast.

Currently they seem to be stuck, but they are still pushing. When they become unstuck, we will have an earthquake that may earn the title, "The Big One!"

Check your supplies and your plan. Now is the time to prepare!

Earthquake Zone!

If you have ever taken the time to actually read those newspaper articles about the likelihood of a major earthquake off our coast, then you've read about tectonic plates. Tectonic plates are those giant puzzle pieces that make up the earth's crust that are constantly in motion, rubbing against each other and creating havoc when they collide or try to slide past one another. The colliding and sliding past isn't so bad, it's when they collide, push, build tension, then suddenly release that causes an earthquake. If the sudden release is at sea, then a tsunami is generated and we all remember watching the videos of Japan's tsunami after their earthquake on March 11, 2011.

Even as we speak, two tectonic plates are entangled in a dance off our coast that will result in a cataclysmic upheaval which will result in an earthquake the likes of which we have never seen.

In January 1700 a similar quake rocked the entire northwest. That was 100 years before Lewis & Clark found their way to the mouth of the Columbia River. Before any white man showed up with a clipboard to keep records of what happened. The Japanese, of course were keeping records and recorded an orphan tsunami which wiped out a portion of their coast, washing at least one fishing village out to sea. It wasn't until just recently estuary core samples revealed major tsunami activity along the Oregon and Washington coasts at that same time. It has been determined that the entire coastline of Oregon and Washington had dropped anywhere between three and ten feet. Farther up north red cedar stumps can be found in salt water marshes along the coast. Everybody knows red cedar trees don't grow in salt water so logic says "something" had to happen to lower the landscape enough so that those stumps are now surrounded by salt water.

Some of those same experts have determined that the Juan de Fuca tectonic plate is pushing its way under the Continental plate. This part is normal, but when the plates get hung up on each other, there is a tension generated which bends the entire plate. Some have likened this to pushing a fishing rod along the ground until it hangs up on something. Sooner or later something lets go and great energy is released. Such will be the case when the two plates off our coast let loose. I should also add that the experts stress this is not a matter of "if", but most certainly a matter of "when."

This set of facts is the best reason I can think of for prepping. When this quake strikes, there will be no roads in and out of our entire region. Bridges closed, highways blocked and busted pavement will shape our travel plans for weeks. Grocery stores will be sold out within hours of the event with no means to replenish. Electrical grid down for weeks on end and the emergency responders unable to answer your 911 calls which aren't going through anyway because all cell phone systems are down as well.

Now is the time to store up some food, supplies and check out your camping gear.

Is that old camp stove still working? Lantern, candles, extra water? If you have a generator, will it start? Do you have enough gas to run it as long as you need it?

After the Shaking

I personally have only experienced one minor earthquake. What I remember is that my recliner was moving from side to side for no reason. About that time my wife commented that "we're having an earthquake!" I walked in to the dining room and we both watched the chandelier over the table sway back and forth. What I marveled at was that everything I had ever considered solid, stable and unshakable, wasn't. I hadn't realized it until then, but my whole paradigm of conscious living was based on the earth being solid. It was pretty unsettling to discover otherwise. All you transplanted Californians are old hands at this, but we Oregonians don't exactly have our sea legs just yet.

I was recently reminded of a very good tip. Keep a fair-sized trash bag under your bed that contains a flashlight, a warm shirt, pants and a good heavy pair of shoes. Secure the bag's draw-strings to the leg of your bed so that you always know where it is. Push the bag under your bed and forget about it, until you need it. Folks underestimate the amount of breakage that can occur during a quake. Running through your house in the dark barefooted is not what you want to do with broken glass all over the place.

Previously we learned what to do during a quake. This time we're going to take a look at what to do after the earth stops moving. Wait until the movement stops. If you're inside a building, get out when it's safe to do so. Spending the day at the beach? Get to high ground, and quickly. In fact, make up your mind right now to act quickly! Depending on the location and severity of the earthquake, you may only have ten minutes to get out of the tsunami zone.

Once you've determined that you're ok, then look for others that need your help. You have just become a first responder. The police, fire and emergency medical personnel are going to busy elsewhere, so you're it! How about your neighbors that may need help? Are there seniors with mobility needs? How about families with infants or special needs children. I covered this earlier about mapping your neighborhood. If you have done all that, then you already know who will need assistance.

Along the way check the homes that have natural gas or propane. Inspect the control valves just in case there are any leaks. This is exactly why all the literature tells you not to light matches or candles following an earthquake and why they tell you to keep a wrench handy.

One more thought; an old saying about keeping your head while all around you others are losing theirs, is wisdom worth having. You can train yourself not to panic; your survival depends on it. The survival of others may well depend on your ability to keep your head about you. Determining *now* what action to take when the occasion arises will save time and quite possibly the lives of your neighbors when the time comes.

One news commentator recently noted that in the event of a Cascadia subduction zone earthquake, Portlanders and others in the Willamette Valley should prepare to survive on their own for at least three weeks. He went on to recommend that those living along the Oregon Coast should prepare for four weeks, or more, of disruption.

Experts believe if an earthquake strikes the northwest, depending, of course, on the location and intensity, all travel in to and out of the area could be cut off. Bridges quite likely will be damaged. Landslides could block roads due to liquefaction and downed trees and other debris will further contribute to the chaos. Electrical power distribution will be interrupted for a lengthy period and grocery supply networks will be at a standstill. The only channels for delivering supplies to the area will likely be by helicopter or by sea. Either mode of supply replenishment will take time to organize and deliver to our area. If the entire Northwest is involved, then the airlift would likely among the largest we've seen in recent history.

Evacuation

Those who prowl the websites, forums and blogs of other preppers will find an entire subculture of otherwise normal people. People who have elevated disaster preparedness to a science or an alternative lifestyle. Terms such as "bugging-out" or "T.E.O.T.W.A.W.K.I." are common lingo. Discussions about firearms, pickup loads of ammo and fortified hidey-holes somewhere in the mountains are concepts routinely bandied about.

Bugging out is also referred to as evacuating. (You remember that from watching all those reruns of M.A.S.H.) T.E.O.T.W.A.W.K.I. is short for "The End Of The World As We Know It." Evacuation is only necessary when it is imminently likely that your humble abode will no longer be "abode-able". Maybe your house is on fire, maybe there is a wildfire on the way, or maybe Hurricane Katrina is bearing down on you. Or as some experienced just recently, the rains have swollen the streams to the point where your home is in imminent flood danger and you are ordered to evacuate.

T.E.O.T.W.A.W.K.I. can occur through natural disaster, economic or societal meltdown, coronal mass ejections (solar storms) or simply the expiration of the Mayan calendar.

Some experts suggest the need for three evacuation plans. A 60 second plan, a one hour plan and a twelve hour plan. So let's pretend you wake in the middle of the night with the smell of smoke in your house. After much panic, screaming and frantic rushing about, (not to mention R-rated language) you get your family and pets out of the house, hopefully without injury. That's an example of the need for a 60 second plan. I have a theory that the panic and screaming factor will be reduced in direct correlation to how much you planning you have done.

On the other hand if the authorities tell you a wildfire is headed your way or the flood waters are rising and you have one hour to get out, you still need a plan. Again, more planning equals less panic and screaming, which equals less stress on the marriage. What to take, what to leave behind, who to notify and oh yes, where to go. When considering where to go, consider this, there is a term for someone who leaves their home with hopes of escaping to some unknown place of 'better-ness'. They're called refugees.

The 12 hour plan is also known as the "Just in Case" plan. "C'mon honey lets gas up the car, and stock up on toilet paper, just in case." This also gives you time to sit down make a list, (if you don't already have one) empty the fridge, unplug your big screen TV, your computer and even flip the master breaker switch on your panel. But then those things should already be in your plan. All in all, we can diminish the damage from a natural disaster and better our chances of survival by simply taking some time to "Make a Plan."

Evacuation: To Go Or Not To Go

There is a concept among preppers known as "Bugging Out." I remember the term from watching reruns of M.A.S.H. Whenever Radar O'Reilly, Major Henry Blake and Hawkeye were ordered to move their Mobile And Surgical Hospital unit to a new location, they would make plans to "bug out." Today's preppers use the term to describe an evacuation process to be executed when the current abode becomes too dangerous to stay put or uninhabitable.

The likelihood of evacuation in our area is usually minor. Our weather events don't equal the hurricanes of the East Coast and Gulf Coast states. Nor do we get the blizzards of the northern regions of our country. We have had isolated instances of evacuation due to flooding and landslides in the past, and for those living in the tsunami inundation zone, bugging out could certainly become a reality.

You can be assured if I lived in a major city or in the hurricane zone, my preparation plans would include how to get my family and supplies out of town on short notice. (Or in prepper lingo, "Out of Dodge.") Living in rural Oregon we have several things to our advantage. Our relatively sparse population is far more self-sufficient and more good-neighbor minded than big city folks. If you've ever watched the news during a big storm or hurricane in a dense-population area, you see all manner of looting and other outlaw behavior.

There seems to be a segment of society always on the cusp of criminal behavior. This group of potential criminals allow themselves to be drawn over the line of unacceptable behavior at the slightest provocation and pillage, loot and even worse when they know the police have their hands full with other matters. You can bet your emergency generator this group has never laid in an extra flashlight battery or can of Spam. Their "plan" such as it is, will be to take your supplies in the event of a disaster. This is precisely why, if I lived in a metropolitan area, I would be planning to "get out of Dodge" if necessary.

If you have relatives or loved ones in the big cities, send them a copy of this and suggest they make plans to 'bug out' if the need arises.

When it is no longer safe to live in your home, then it's time to evacuate. Some evacuations are middle-of-the-night, grab what you can and run because the water heater just set the house on fire. But more often we think of evacuating in the face of a hurricane, tornado, or other cataclysmic event. Then there are the times that you have a little more warning. In past columns, I haven't dwelt too much on evacuation because in our region, hurricanes and tornadoes are just not that common.

Wildfires forced evacuations in Southern Oregon during last year's fire season. According to officials, some were more "disaster-ready" than others. Each family was told to consider the 5 "P's" when making plans to evacuate. The 5 "P's" include People and Pets (and other livestock), Papers (important documents), Prescriptions, including hearing aids, eyeglasses and your medications, Photographs, so your memories are preserved and last is your Personal Computer. There is often invaluable, irreplaceable data on your hard drive.

Of course, having a complete 72 hour kit at the ready is going to ease the task of what to take, but as always having a plan in place will eliminate a whole lot of confusion when the time comes to evacuate. When you have a plan, the panic factor, not to mention the stress on the marriage, is greatly diminished.

Home Fire Safety

Often when we think of disaster preparedness, we think in terms of earthquake, massive storm or major power outages. The concept of disaster gets more personal when there is a home fire. Everyone knows someone who has lost everything in a house fire. I have spoken to two people within the last several weeks that have had their own private disaster when fire destroyed their homes and all their belongings. Happily, both parties were quick to add that, "At least no one was hurt."

Last year fire departments in the U.S. responded to 370,000 home fires resulting in nearly 14,000 injuries and 2,520 civilian deaths. Damages in the amount of $6.9 billion occurred as a result. Here are some other facts regarding fires in the home:

Most fires start in the kitchen from cooking accidents. (42%) Home structure fires peak around the dinner hour, between 5:00 and 8:00 PM.

Seven percent of home fires start in the bedroom, most often from smoking. These fires caused 25% of home fire deaths.

Nearly two-thirds (62%) of home fire deaths resulted from fires in homes with no smoke alarms or no working smoke alarms.

The good news is that for the past 35 years, the trend is improving. In 1977 there were 723,500 home fires resulting in 5,865 deaths. Every year there have been fewer fires and fewer fatalities. Today those number are less than half what they were.

Safety tips are always available from your local fire department, but some things to keep in mind include, keep fresh batteries in your smoke alarms, usually once a year will do it. Some folks use their birthdays as reminders, and some use January 1, but whichever method you prefer, just do it! If you need smoke alarms, buy them. They are simple to test, simple to use and simple to install.

For those who burn wood for heat, now would be a good time to get your chimney inspected and cleaned. Soot and creosote can build up in your flue and ignite, rapidly involving your entire house.

For kitchen safety, stay in the room if frying, grilling or broiling food. If you leave the kitchen, even for a short time, turn off the stove. A leading contributor of fires in the kitchen is unattended cooking. Keep a lid nearby when you're cooking to smother small grease fires.

Fire prevention can be practiced by everyone and in most cases it's not a case of disaster preparedness, but rather disaster prevention! I'll take that any day.

Fire Season

Already this weekend, I have heard the fire siren go off at least three times summoning our volunteer department to respond to someone's personal disaster. According to the American Red Cross, home fires are the biggest disaster threat in the United States. The Red Cross responds to a fire in someone's home about every eight minutes. Home fires are more prevalent than floods, hurricanes, and tornadoes. Simply by following a few simple safety rules you can drastically reduce the danger of fire in your home.

Before I start with safety rules, I want to mention a couple of pieces of equipment. First are your smoke detectors. The Red Cross recommends having a working smoke detector on every level of your home and in every bedroom. Test them each month by pushing the little button and while you're at it, get the kids in on the act to teach them what the alarm sounds like and what means if they hear it go off. Then pick one special day each year to replace the batteries. Or at least listen for the little chirp that signals an almost dead battery and swap out the battery right away.

Secondly, how many of you actually have a fire extinguisher in your home? Before you run out and buy a supply of fire extinguishers for home use, stop by the local fire department for suggestions on the right type (usually a Class A,B,C) and instructions for proper use.

And for those of you non-NRA types, who are opposed to using guns for home defense, if the occasion arises and you need to defend yourself and your family, just hose the perp down with your fire extinguisher. Besides being 100% legal to have in your home, you can purchase one without a permit, (or a background check) and it will incapacitate an attacker by making him unable to breathe, see or even hear anything.

Electric heaters; get the kind that turn off automatically when they tip over. Also never leave them running when you leave the house or go to sleep. Talk to your kids regularly about the dangers of fire and the misuse of matches and lighters. Keep them out of reach of small children. And here's one for the "duh" category; Never smoke in bed! For a more complete list, go to www.redcross.org. There is a printable checklist on their website.

Don't forget to have a fire escape plan. Not only should your plan include alternate routes to get out of the house but a common gathering point needs to be established as well. And finally if your power goes out and the temperature in your home is dropping, DO NOT use a charcoal grill for warmth. Every year I read of some bonehead who brought the charcoal grill in the house and tragedy ensued. Carbon monoxide kills!

If you burn wood for heat, have your chimney inspected and cleaned, if necessary. Don't cut corners when so much is at stake.

Holiday Preparedness

My mother had a saying, "Christmas comes the same time every year, two weeks too early!" She was an elementary teacher and there were always parties, programs, pageants and presents for which to prepare. This year seems no different. December's calendar fills up pretty quickly and the big day will be upon us in no time.

Every year I read of Christmas tragedy in the form of house fires. Make sure your home and family are safe this and every holiday season by following a few simple safety rules. Inspect your Christmas tree lighting for worn wiring, overloaded circuits and and if you are still using those screw-in bulbs, make sure there are no broken bulbs or exposed filaments. One of every three Christmas tree fires is caused by electrical problems. Although Christmas tree fires are not common, when they do occur, they are likely to be serious. On average one of every 40 reported home Christmas tree structure fires results in a death compared to an average of one death per 142 totals reported structure fires. A heat source too close to the tree causes one of six reported Christmas tree fires.

More than half (56%) of home candle fires are a result of something flammable situated too close to the flame. There are a significant higher percentage of candle-related fires in December than other months of the year.

If you're still putting up a "real" tree every year, make sure you keep it well-watered. If you've ever burned your tree after Christmas, you know how fast it can go up.

Here are a few more tips from the experts: Keep candles at least 12 inches away from anything that burns. Make sure your tree is at least three feet away from heat sources like fireplaces, radiators, space heaters, candles or heat vents. Get rid of your Christmas tree immediately after the holiday. Connect no more than three strings of mini lights, or no more than 50 lights of the screw-in variety.

Oh and one more thing, keep your fire extinguisher handy. It takes less than 30 seconds for a dry tree to go up in flames. No time to run out to the garage and grab it.

Winter is statistically the worst for home fires. Cold weather coupled with holiday decorations and over-burdened heating and electrical systems boost the danger-factor significantly. Take care of your family this year and walk through your home with "fresh eyes" looking for anything that may cause a fire

Amateur Radio

Ever since Marconi tinkered with wireless transmissions in the early 1900's, people have been fascinated with communicating via the airwaves. Today there are over 700,000 amateur radio licenses issued to private individuals in the U.S. In our rural Oregon county alone there are approximately 300 license holders. Granted not all of those are active, some haven't touched their radio in years and some are simply no longer with us.

Amateur radio operators (also known as "hams") have played a vital role in disaster response for decades. Groups such as A.R.E.S (Amateur Radio Emergency Services) and R.A.C.E.S. (Radio Amateur Civil Emergency Service) are well established and have good working relationships with other local disaster planners. In one small city alone there are ham radio stations set up at the hospital, the City Hall and the Fire Department. In the event of an emergency this equipment is designed to operate free from the electrical grid and would be manned by personnel from A.R.E.S/R.A.C.E.S. Emergency communications networks can keep the local responders informed of developing events, while having the capability of communicating on a global basis. Other cities have similar setups with their amateur radio folks.

One might think with internet technology such as Skype or Facetime, making video calls to loved ones all over the planet, that amateur radio would be relegated to the dustbin of "last millennium technology". Quite the opposite is true. Over the past five years the Federal Communication Commission reports issuing nearly 25,000 new licenses. Digital radio equipment is less expensive and more powerful than ever before. When an earthquake or similar event could sever fiber optic cables and bring down electrical grids, a battery powered ham radio can still transmit and receive vital messages throughout the county and around the world. Even to outer space.

During my time in Viet Nam, every G.I. knew if he wanted to call home, he would simply go to the local M.A.R.S. (Military Amateur Radio Station). The M.A.R.S. folks would make ham radio contact with another ham operator in the States, who would in-turn initiate a collect call to your home then do a "phone-patch" and presto, you could talk to your loved one. Of course half the planet could listen in on your call and after every phrase you had so say "over" so they would know when to key or release the microphone, but it was a touch from home. Those calls were considered invaluable to preserve the sanity of our guys half a world away living in unspeakable conditions. So on behalf of a multitude of Viet Nam Veterans, I'd like to extend thanks to all those amateur radio operators we never got to meet or thank in person.

Following is an email sent to me by a reader regarding an incident some years back in which amateur radio played an active role in a disaster right here in Coos County: *My Dad, and I were the only communications between Myrtle Point and the outside world in December 1955 during the West Coast floods. Myrtle Point was isolated by floods toward Coquille and slides between the Powers Junction and Roseburg, and the phone lines were out too. During that time, John Cawrse in Remote managed to get a short phone call through to tell me that a slide had covered a home just east of Remote. Since the Oregon Emergency Net (an Oregon network of Ham Radio operators) was mobilized during the emergency, I was able to contact a fellow ham in Roseburg and he put together a caravan of an ambulance and a bulldozer on a truck, as well as the ham, (Don, W7SHA), to try to get to Remote for a rescue. Don had a "mobile rig" in his car and he accompanied them and kept in touch with us to report their progress. As I recall, it took them most of the night to get there, unloading the bulldozer at several slides and clearing the road to get to the scene of the accident. Sadly, all the residents of the home were deceased.*

(Editorial research discovered there were actually two survivors in the house.)

Dad and I both received a "Public Service" award from the American Radio Relay League for our communications during that time and I still have mine in my records. I am still a licensed ham and still active on the Oregon Emergency Net when we are in the Oregon area, to maintain that emergency preparedness.

Again, thanks for the memories!

Thanks for the story, Bob.

Even in this day of internet and cell phone high tech communications, ham radio is every bit as relevant as it was in 1955. If the power grid were to collapse in time of earthquake, it is likely the cell phone system would be rendered inoperable as well. Ham radio does require electricity, but many hams are set up to run off alternate power sources such as solar, generators and vehicle electrical systems. For this reason many first responder agencies have forged partnerships with the amateur radio community. Hams will be pressed into service to provide communications with other agencies and with the outside world. A well-equipped amateur radio operator can bounce signals off the moon and communicate with hams on the other side of the planet. To combine a hobby with a needed service during times of disaster is rewarding indeed.

What's On The Menu

We were having one of our winter storms, the kind where the rain is coming down sideways and the trees are bending back and forth. I was at work 20 miles from home when my wife called and announced that the electricity had gone out and wanted to know where I had stored our camp stove. It was in my shop and I told her how to find it.

A short time later, I received another phone call, this one with a bit more volume behind it, if you know what I mean. She found the stove right where I said it was. What I had neglected to warn her of, you see, was that there were at least two killer mice living inside the box where it was stored. (I seriously did not know this ahead of time, really!) As she described it, both mice ran down her arm and escaped into the nether regions of my shop. But not before doing irreparable damage to her mouse-aphobia. You can imagine her delight as she related the story. That was about when I asked if the mice were ok...but that's another story.

Arriving home, I fully expected to dine on canned chili or beef stew. Much to my surprise she had fixed pork chops, mashed potatoes, gravy and vegetables for dinner that night on our little Coleman stove.

Not all 'survival' meals are going to measure up to that one. But with a little planning and not a whole lot of extra expense, you can build up a decent pantry to draw from during a disaster.

About this time I know what you're thinking, "I'll just go to the store and get what I need after the lights go out." Bad plan! You can expect there will be a run on the store, besides in the event of a substantial disaster; experts believe most stores will be emptied out within four hours. In the event of a major earthquake in our region, we can plan to go several days, possibly weeks before our local stores are resupplied.

Now is a good time to mention that if all the power in the region is out, you won't be able to rely on your debit or credit card to cover your purchases. Some, not all grocery stores will have generator power to keep their refrigerated inventory cold, but if the banks are all shut down no one is going to honor your plastic. Stores may be operating on a cash-only basis. So it's a good idea to have a bit of cash set aside to cover expenses under those conditions. How much cash you keep on hand is up to you and your budget.

Now when you're stocking up, it's a good idea to buy things you can prepare just by mixing with hot water. Soup mixes are a good choice, especially in colder weather. If you think about it, most power outages come in the middle of a wind-rain storm. Ideal soup weather! Kids love Ramen noodles, they're not all that nutritious, but they are inexpensive and easy to fix. So a case or two of Top Ramen really isn't a bad idea

Secondly, buy foods that you are accustomed to eating. There is no benefit to throwing your body into a gastric crisis because you suddenly have only MREs to eat. (MRE:
Meals, Ready to Eat, used by the military when out in the field, away from a 'real' mess hall.) Or you have only stocked up on freeze-dried backpacking fare without ever trying one out. You are already in a stressful situation, your body knows it and will likely revolt if you suddenly change your diet. Is now a good time to suggest buying some anti-diarrhea medicine?

Watch the sales, stock up slowly, use coupons, "buy-one-get-one" sales and try to get items you are already accustomed to serving your family. Freeze-dried, dehydrated food will help you survive, but how much your kids grumble about it, now that's another matter.

Preparedness Gardening

Whenever the economy does a downturn the seed companies experience an upturn. Planting a vegetable garden is viewed by many as one way to push back against high food prices and an uncertain economy. Many preppers consider a garden as a hedge against not only high prices but the inability of the grocery supply line to come through in the event of a disaster or other interruption in the supply chain.

Obviously gardening is a long-term project not to be rolled out the day after an earthquake with the expectation of a ready food supply. If you've never tried growing your own vegetables it can be not only a rewarding hobby but could potentially feed your family if needed. Something to consider before you plow up your backyard is the raised-bed concept of gardening. Build a raised-bed enables you to confine your garden space to a specific area controlled by the framework of the raised bed. Other benefits include the ability to control the soil or planting medium you prefer, enhanced draining ability, and raised beds tend to warm up faster, possibly giving you a jump on the planting season. There are plenty of books and on-line resources to glean for information about raised-bed gardening.

Another item to consider is a sprout kit. A sprout kit usually contains a variety of seeds suitable for raising edible sprouts. There are several versions available and most come with the hydroponic growing apparatus needed to raise healthy, nutritious, organic sprouts. Sprouts can be grown in just a few days and are rich in vitamins, minerals, trace elements, enzymes and fiber. They provide a quick supply of vegetables for use in salads, sandwiches and stir-fry. They may be steamed and even used in some baked goods. Prices for a sprout kit run in the $50-$80 range, depending on which model you prefer.

So while you're laying in supplies, don't forget that vegetable gardening can take you just one more step closer to the independence necessary for surviving calamity

Chicken Farmer

For the past three years, I have purchased baby chicks in hopes of starting some kind of productive (and successful) poultry program. This is not my first attempt at chicken farming. (Or is it ranching?) The first year I started with nine and lost them over a period of months mostly to murderous raccoons. I woke up on the morning of December 24 and discovered the last five had all been killed the night before. Two months later, determined to get it right, I ordered another batch. (Did you know they're shipped through the U.S. Mail?) This time I started with nearly two dozen chicks. Over the next several months they were slowly picked off by raccoons, but mostly by the neighbor's dog. The final ones were killed sometime around the first of the year. This time I think I've got all the holes plugged in my fence and the neighbor's dog seems to be no longer a factor, especially since mine weren't the only chickens he feasted on. No further comment. So maybe the third time's the charm?

If you're interested in disaster preparedness, then maybe you should consider chickens as a part of your plan. First of all once they mature, they provide a steady supply, and sometimes an overabundant supply, of fresh eggs. Everybody knows once you've had farm fresh eggs; it ruins you for the store-bought variety. A little bit like home-canned tuna versus store bought tuna. Some folks even get a rooster and work at hatching their own chicks, thus perpetuating your flock. No you don't need a rooster to get eggs, only if you want those eggs to hatch into baby chicks. If that confuses you, then you need to ask your mom to review "the talk"! Then some raise chicks especially to butcher. There are some varieties that gain weight very quickly and can be butchered in six to eight weeks time. Certain breeds are better for laying eggs, and still some are a good cross between both types. The feed store where I bought my last batch of chicks orders in the most popular breeds, among which are Rhode Island Reds, Barred Rocks and Buff Orpingtons. If you research what kind of chicks you want, the feed store will order them for you or you can order them directly and eliminate the middleman. Some hatcheries require a minimum order so if you're just testing the waters, you may want to start small and buy from the local feed store. Another advantage to doing business locally is they have the waterers, feeders and the proper feed to start your little peepers. Most chickens start laying in 20 to 24 weeks so there is a pretty fair time lag to production. Once they start laying you might just wind up with more than you can eat so you'll find your neighbors, relatives and fellow church-goers are happy to take them off your hands.

Food Supplies

Getting a kit together is a lot like planning for a camping trip. Let's see, we're going to be gone for six days so we'll have to take food for 18 meals, plus snacks, s'mores ingredients and drinks. Then comes the sleeping bags, extra clothes, tent, camping stove and on and on and on. The only difference between packing for a camping trip and preparing for a major disaster is with the latter, we really don't know how long to plan for. Those living in Hurricane Sandy territory were still without some services up to 60 days following the arrival of the storm. By that time F.E.M.A. had arrived and other services, including food were brought in from outside the area.

I have read that grocery stores in the region were sold out within three to four hours; there were similar reports from other stores dealing in camping gear and supplies. Someone recently approached me and asked about food resources locally. Although there are a few food banks in the area, they really are not set up to serve our entire region in the event an earthquake strikes our region. The food banks receive supplies either from donated sources, program funding from various agencies which can be affected by the ebb and flow of available money or the generosity of local food drives and private individuals. These food banks routinely provide groceries to families in need in our communities. There is no cache of groceries in our county set aside specifically to be distributed in the event of a disaster.

Back in the Civil Defense days of the 1950s to 1960s, there were some resources on hand to be "activated" in case of enemy attack. There was an entire military field hospital stored in one of the buildings at our local airport. This unit contained everything, with the exception of medications and staff, needed to set up a Mobile And Surgical Hospital (M.A.S.H.). That unit was dismantled sometime in the late 1970s. There are currently no government (or private) warehouses full of food in our area to be distributed in case of disaster.

So now we're back to the Y.O.Y.O. scene. You're On Your Own! Building a pantry doesn't require a huge extra outlay of funds. Start by watching the sales. Take advantage of the 'buy one get one' bargains. One lady wrote to me and bragged she had saved $8000 in a year's time by using coupons, online bargains and shopping the sales. The side benefit was she had built up a very tidy stockpile of groceries as she did so.

If money is no object, there are literally hundreds (or more) websites selling disaster preparedness food supplies. You can order freeze-dried, dehydrated, canned or a combination of all the above. Some even offer free shipping. A word of caution, all the experts recommend storing food that you are accustomed to eating. During times of emergency, your body is already stressed and introducing an entirely foreign diet could result in some unpleasant gastric distress.

Jump Starting Your Food Supply

Whenever a person thinks of prepping, the first topic that usually comes to mind is food. What to store, how much to store, how to store, and which store to go to? There are all kinds of food packages you can purchase. You can get a year's supply of dehydrated or freeze-dried fare for $4,000 or a 72 hour kit for one person at WalMart for $64.00.

Following is a list of items you can buy at your local grocery store, things that you would probably have on hand anyway. The dehydrated kits you buy generally tout a 25-year shelf life. So the normal things you purchase, should be rotated out every few months or so. One rule of thumb when it comes to storing up food is; buy food that your body is accustomed to eating!

Some people lay in backpacking, freeze-dried food to be eaten when the time comes. That is all well and good, unless you have never tried those entrees and you experience a revolt of sorts when you're already stressed out anyway. Store food to which your body is already accustomed!

Here's your shopping list:

1. 20 lbs of rice. Rice seems pretty boring, but it is filling, nutritious and adaptable to a wide variety of entrees.

2. 20 lbs of pinto beans. Beans are also a valuable part of every storage plan. Combined with rice they fulfill a protein need in your menu.
3. 20 cans of vegetables. Green beans, peas, corn and canned tomatoes are a good start. Buy what you already eat and enjoy.
4. 20 cans of fruit. Peaches, pears, pineapple, fruit cocktail, all to your taste.
5. 20 cans of meat. Chicken, tuna, shrimp, salmon, Vienna sausages, beef stew and don't forget Spam. Those square cans fit really well on the shelf and if it's fried, you can make the kids believe it is "camping bacon." It worked for my kids anyway. I even recently found some canned roast beef.
6. 4 lbs of oats. A warm bowl of oatmeal can be a welcome meal any time of day. Topped with some canned fruit, it makes a refreshing treat.
7. 2 (or more) large jars of peanut butter. A good source of protein and surprisingly filling. Tastes good too!
8. Pick up a supply of powdered drink mix. Tang, Crystal Light or similar product. Make sure it's loaded with vitamin C.
9. 5 lbs of powdered milk. It's great protein and is loaded with other nutrients. It's filling and can be used on that oatmeal as well.

10. 5 lbs of salt. Salt is an essential for survival as well as a food enhancer. Our bodies need salt to survive.
11. 10 lbs of pancake mix. Buy the "just add water" variety, such as Krusteaz. Simple to make, easy to fix and everybody's familiar with hotcakes. Don't forget a jug of syrup
12. 2 lbs of honey and 2 jars of jam. Everybody needs a little sweetness.
13. 10 lbs of pasta. Again, easy to fix, familiar to everyone and a great comfort food.
14. 10 cans or jars of spaghetti sauce. Goes great with the pasta. Cheap and satisfying. It's not homemade, but it does dress up the pasta.
15. 20 cans of soup or broth or soup mixes. The beauty of soup is that they are a budget friendly, all-in-one meal solution and most require only water for preparation.
16. 1 large jug of cooking oil. Olive oil, vegetable oil, coconut or some other cooking oil, but definitely get some.
17. Spices and condiments. "Spice" up your pasta and oatmeal with some of the spices you already have in your cupboard and are accustomed to using, but lay in some extra. Garlic, pepper, Tabasco, all your favorites.

18. 5 lbs of coffee and 100 tea bags. For some of us life just isn't life without our coffee. Tea can be therapeutic and soothing as well.
19. 2 large bags of hard candies. Peppermints, butterscotch and lemon drops can go a long way toward making a hard situation bearable.
20. Flashlight and extra batteries. Lots of extra batteries. Ok, I know, this isn't edible. But you can never have enough flashlights and batteries.

Now I know what you're saying. There are a lot of essentials I forgot. Remember this is a "starter" list. Some might say we need flour, wheat, yeast, and other baking necessities. Quite frankly a whole lot of folks today don't have a clue what to do with flour, nor do they have an oven that works without electricity. Those things, and others, are important and should be a part of every food plan so don't pass them by when working your comprehensive plan.

When the Lights Go Out

I am always impressed at how well our electricity stays on, especially during some of our big wind storms. But we all know that every so often, our power goes out for one reason or another. A transformer blows, a tree comes down across a line somewhere, or a drunk driver takes out a power pole. Whatever the reason, we are sometimes left in the dark. That's when we grab a flashlight, start looking for those candles and drag out the Coleman lantern.

That's also when we walk into a darkened room and out of habit flip the light switch. Then we feel just a wee bit silly and hope nobody else noticed. Admit it, we've all done it. I thought so.

So let's talk about emergency generators. Should you buy one, which one do you need? Can you justify the expense? How much gasoline should you store? Here's my take on the subject. I own a generator, but I don't consider it a long term solution. Three or four days maybe a week at the most. The reason? They require fuel. Most are gasoline powered; some are propane, some diesel and some even use natural gas. But few of us can, or are willing, to store up that much gasoline. For short-term use, a generator can mean the difference between keeping your fridge running and throwing out a bunch of spoiled food. It can also supply electricity to pump water out of your well.

If you make the decision to buy a generator, here are some things to keep in mind. Consider the wattage output. How many watts do you need? If you buy a 4000 watt unit, what can you expect that it will power up? Here's a little table to help:

	Starting wattage	Running wattage
Refrigerator	1600	200
TV (tube)	300	300
TV (flat screen)	190	190
Coffee maker	600	600
Dishwasher (cool dry)	540	216
Clothes washer	1200	1200
Dryer	6750	5400 (requires 240 volt)
Water Heater	4500	4500 (requires 240 volt)

Much more information is available online, but you get the idea. You can't expect to power up your entire home on a 4000 watt generator.

Now a couple of things not to do with a generator. Don't leave it running in an enclosed area, like your attached garage or back porch or basement. The reason? Carbon monoxide will kill you. Secondly, some ingenious types have figured out that if you wire a male plug to both ends of an extension cord, you can plug into any outlet and power up your house. This is a bad idea for several reasons. You could overload your generator and possibly burn it out, you could heat up your electrical circuits causing a fire hazard and most importantly it is a danger to utility workers. When a worker is repairing a line he thinks is dead and Harry Homeowner has plugged a generator into the system it will energize the line he is working on. I'm no electrician but I'm told when 240 volts passes backwards through the transformer into the power grid, it becomes 24,000 volts. My numbers may not be accurate, but the principle is correct. Understandably utility companies really frown on this practice. Don't do it!

The best thing about generators is they give us the ability to function with some normalcy when the power company fails. Generator owners exude a certain smugness knowing they can still function, to a degree, when all others have just been relegated to the Stone Age. The generator owners I know don't realize they're being smug, nor do they purposely conduct themselves with an air of superiority, but it's there. Trust me.

If you have been considering joining this exclusive club of generator owners, first ask yourself some questions. What do I plan to do with it? Am I going to just power up my travel trailer when I'm camping or do I intend to provide electricity for my home when the power goes out?

The power company does an amazing job of keeping the electricity flowing, especially during our winter wind and rain storms. How those lines stay attached to their poles and keep the juice running is a marvel of engineering. We all know there are times when things happen and service is interrupted. Sometimes things get fixed right away and sometimes its days before the lights come back on. It's those times when it takes more than a day or so that you need a generator. You've got to pump water out of your well, keep your refrigerator and freezer cold, or in some cases open your garage door.

Here are some things to keep in mind. Unless you're in the position to spend upwards of $15,000 for a permanently mounted unit, don't plan to energize your whole house. A smaller, portable unit of 4000 watt capacity will handle your fridge, freezer, a few lights and your TV. The cost for a unit like that will be in the $500-800 range. The bigger the wattage output, the more the unit will handle. Like everything else, you get what you pay for. Avoid the $99.00 2-cycle unit. It will probably do more damage (like to your computer or to your $2000 flat-screen TV) than it does good. And while we're on the topic, a high quality surge suppressor is a really good bit of insurance for your delicate electronics.

The main drawback with generators is the fuel situation. Don't plan on using your generator as a long-term solution. Even running the unit only a few hours a day for more than a week, you'd need to store more stabilized fuel than most budgets allow. Not to mention the inherent dangers of storing gasoline. Speaking of gasoline, today's ethanol-infused product presents its own problem. Ethanol naturally attracts water, thus dramatically shortening the storage life of gasoline. A generator sitting idle for months on end will almost surely fail to start because of bad gasoline. The solution is to purchase non-ethanol gas (at a much higher price) or using a product such as Sta-Bil (Marine-grade if you can get it) to keep fuel fresh for 12 months or longer.

Here's an excellent resource for generator information. Go to Amazon.com, and click on their "Patio, Lawn & Garden" section. Then choose "generators" and then find the "buying guide" link. They have posted lots of great information on the topic of buying a generator. For instance, a transfer switch is highly recommended. Transfer switches are pre-wired to your breaker panel, usually by an electrician. They prioritize which electrical circuits will be energized when the generator is in use. Deciding on whether or not to install a power transfer switch should be one of your first priorities. Otherwise you are relegated to running extension cords from your generator to the appliances you wish to power up.

Among the things I have learned from experience are: My generator isn't big enough to power up my entire house. Choose which items you want to run, and run extension cords to them lastly, make sure your generator is completely outside. Gasoline engines emit carbon monoxide and can kill you and your family if you've decided to keep it in the attached garage.

Many mid-priced generators now are equipped with electric starters, a nice option to consider if tugging on a starter rope isn't exactly your cup of tea. Also, a must-have item is a wheel kit. Otherwise you will lift it, lug it or slide it to where it is going to be used. Wheel kits make the job so much easier. Moving it into place is as simple as using a wheelbarrow.

Getting Home

I read somewhere that "The best kit is the one you have with you." We can have our homes prepared to the max, but if we aren't home when disaster strikes, it does us little good. It was November 18, 1996. I was at work at my post office some 40 miles from home. As I recall, it was raining when I got up that day, but by mid-morning it *really* began to rain, in earnest. Along with the rain high winds swept in off the ocean and before long we had one of the most vicious storms I had seen. The rain-swollen streams began to sweep all manner of debris along with the water and soon clogged culverts, flooding the roads. By mid-afternoon it was apparent there was no let-up and I began to hear reports that the highway may close down. I need that particular stretch of highway to get home. After I closed the post office and started home, I made it about ten miles before the highway department turned me around. I had no choice but to head back to my post office and prepare to spend the night. I had previously stashed a sleeping bag, a shaving kit and a few cans of non-perishable food at the post office.

I stopped by the local market to get some more groceries, when the owner of the market asked if I was going to be able to get home. He invited me to bunk in at his house that night. In fact, he wouldn't take no for answer. We cooked a batch of spaghetti for dinner and later when the crew from the power company showed up, we cooked dinner for them. My point is that I wasn't completely unprepared; although I was pleased I didn't have to spend the night on the floor of the post office.

If I had my way, any disaster would take place while my family and I are comfortably at home. But we can't schedule storms or earthquakes, the reality is now I work closer to home, but it is still a 20 mile drive, and spend eight or more hours a day in my office there. My wife spends all day at her job in 30 miles from the nest. The likelihood of at least one of us being stranded away from home in an emergency is very good. So let's play a game of "Let's Pretend." If you were stranded in another city during a disaster, would you have what you need with you to get by? And oh by the way, all the stores are closed and the ATMs won't work because the power is out.

If you ask most people, "What would you do if you were in another city during an emergency?" Most people would say, "I'd get home as soon as possible." Have you considered that you just might not be able to get home? Trees, power poles, power lines, building debris, massive traffic jam with everybody else trying to do the same thing, bridges out, and roads flooded are all realistic reasons why your best option may be to sit it out for a few hours. If the emergency is an earthquake, make sure you're out of the tsunami zone and sit tight. If you have your kit with you, you're good.

So what's in a kit? Everyone's kit will look different depending on your specific needs. We all have the same four basic needs: (1) food, (2) water, (3) shelter, and (4) security. (Maslow's hierarchy of need notwithstanding.) Good, strong walking shoes are a must, if you take some kind of maintenance medication, then you should have your meds with you, at least three or four days worth. It's called a "Get Home Bag". Yours will look different than mine, but water, food and shelter are the basics. Some extra clothes, but the shoes you wear to work are probably not the ones you want to wear to walk any distance. Get a bag, get started and just imagine what you'd do if you were stranded some distance from home.

Gadgets and Gizmos

My family calls me a "gadget freak". I confess, I love gadgets. I admit to having three GPS receivers. I also confess to once building a solar-powered cell phone charger that fit in an Altoids tin. Ads for survival knives, or solar-powered, hand-crank radios are everywhere and they always catch my attention. (And yes, I own at least two of each.) Every workable disaster preparedness kit not only contains food, but should have some equipment as well. In many cases, equipment equals gadgets.

The get-home bag I carry at all times contains, among other things, some food items a knife, a NOAA weather radio, flashlight, a fire-starting kit and a water filter.

Because water is essential, and because drinking contaminated water can make you very sick, I have a water bottle with a built-in filter. It's designed to fill with water, like from a stream and then when you draw on the tube; it pulls water through the filter, removing all the things that make you sick. I also have a Steri-Pen, an ultraviolet device that purifies water.

Then there's the GPS. Global Positioning Satellite technology still fascinates me. My most recent version was a gift from my son. "Remember Dad, these things are ten percent technology and ninety percent common sense." His warning was based on the numerous mis-steps publicized in the media when people got in trouble when they blindly relied on their GPS. They work great, but for some technical reasons, they can give faulty directions. That doesn't stop me from being fascinated by watching that little pickup go past the same intersection that I am passing or watching the little speed limit sign change at the exact instant I pass the real sign on the highway. I still rely on a GPS when I'm looking for an address in Portland, Medford or Redding. I have yet to be misled. When I take my ATV out in the hills, I record my location when I unload from the pickup, and then go exploring. My GPS always takes me right back to the pickup. Hunters, mushroom pickers and hikers can all benefit from carrying that little device in their shirt pocket.

Another is the Storm Station by Black & Decker. When the power goes out, the first thing I reach for is my Storm Station. It is a keep-it-plugged-in-to-stay-fully-charged radio, detachable flashlight, power supply and auxiliary light. It provides weather information, AM-FM radio and TV audio reception. It has a 12-volt plug in, also a 110 volt outlet. It doesn't have the capacity to power up much, but I always know where it is and therefore I know where I can find a flashlight in the dark.

There are lots of items on the market labeled "survival" or "emergency". As you might imagine not all of them live up to their billing. They may or may not help your situation in a disaster; it's up to your good judgment to sort that out.

Group Prep

Until now the focus has been on family and home preparedness. And while I still believe that should be the individual priority, I am equally convinced that whatever service club or church organization with which you are involved should also be prepared to meet needs when necessary. Historically when a disaster or traumatic event strikes, church attendance swells. It seems to be a pattern anytime there is a crisis; people tend to look to a higher power for stability and comfort. There's not a church in the country that doesn't want to be known as the place that met the needs of its community when disaster happened. Don't get me wrong, I still believe that families need to stock up. Get a kit, make a plan, and be informed, are very viable and essential for home preparedness. But when churches and service clubs are ready, it can make all the difference in your community.

A few years when two major hurricanes struck the Gulf Coast, more than 40,000 refugees fled to the city of Austin, Texas. Several pastors showed up at shelters only to be turned away because they were neither trained nor had any qualifications to deal with the situation. Since then the Red Cross (upon request) has provided training to thousands of pastors and church members in their city. As a result, Austin is now one of the most "ready" cities in America. To date, members of the Austin Disaster Relief Network have been called upon to respond to floods and fires in the surrounding area. Some were even sent to Joplin, Missouri, to assist following the devastating tornado in that area.

Many churches in our region already have some food supplies on hand; some are operating their own mini food bank and most have a commercial-grade kitchen. Moving ahead with an expanded disaster plan, including increasing supplies on hand, would be a small step toward making a big difference. And while you're at it, how about compiling a skills inventory of your group. Who has medical experience? Is there a nurse or doctor in your group? Does anyone have skills in working with children? How about counseling? Maybe a team of musicians that don't need electricity to make music. You get the idea. If this sounds familiar, it should. Your church or service club is a microcosm of the community and it may be every bit as important to map your group, as it is to map your neighborhood.

The next time your service club or church has a planning session, show them a copy of this column. When all the lights in the neighborhood are out except for the Coleman lantern in your gathering place, people will naturally be drawn to you. If there is a pot of soup on the propane stove and some coffee going, you might just make an impression on someone. You could save lives. Food for thought...

To Gun or Not To Gun

I knew once I began the discussion on disaster preparedness, sooner or later the topic of guns would come up. I have purposely avoided the subject because of strong feelings on both sides of the issue but the question has come up, so let's take a look.

The widely accepted opinion is that during times of disaster the police are overwhelmed. Watching looters during times of civil unrest or Hurricane Katrina tells us that a certain element of society will run amok if it is obvious they can loot, pillage and burn with impunity. An old axiom is, "When seconds count, the police are only minutes away!" Considering this, many disaster preppers consider gun ownership as a vital part of their preparations.

Let me say right up front I'm a gun owner. I am a past member of the NRA and consider myself a recreational shooter. As a former police officer, the firearm was simply a tool of the trade. My family grew accustomed to seeing my duty belt (with loaded .357) hanging from the gun rack in our bedroom. But then, not all families are accustomed to having firearms in the home. Not only are they nervous around anything gun related, they are vehemently opposed to anything to do with a firearm.

Gun ownership in the United States is at an all-time high. More people are buying firearms now than at any time in our history. At the same time, violent crimes including murder, rape and armed robbery are at a 30 year low! Coincidence? Author Robert Heinlein once wrote, "An armed society is a polite society."

Attempting to determine how many people own firearms resulted in vague answers. Nationwide, it is estimated the percentage of households owning firearms is somewhere between 39% and 50%. I believe that the percentage in Southwestern Oregon is markedly higher. Just a feeling I have. Of course there are population pockets throughout the U.S. where gun ownership is believed to approach 100%. A more exact statistic is in regard to concealed handgun licenses. Our county currently has on the books over 3800 permits. With a county population of 63,000, 6% of our citizens are licensed to carry a concealed handgun. Statewide there are nearly 147,000 concealed handgun licenses issued.

How you choose to protect your family is your business. The police will likely be unavailable during any significant emergency. If your choice is to purchase a firearm, then that's a decision you shouldn't make lightly. Do your research. Get some training, get some more training, and practice safety!

Stuff About Knives

"Mary gave him a bran-new "Barlow" knife worth twelve and a half cents; and the convulsion of delight that swept his system shook him to his foundations. True, the knife would not cut anything, but it was a "sure-enough" Barlow, and there was inconceivable grandeur in that - ...". - *The Adventures of Tom Sawyer*

Knives have always been a part of American culture. From a rite of passage for Tom Sawyer to today's hi-tech blade systems and multi-tools. Whether or not you carry a knife in your pocket or purse every day, you should have one in your kit. There are folding knives, non-folding knives, multi-bladed knives and all kinds of spring-loaded knives. Big ones, little ones and in-between ones. There's a knife for every purpose and for every budget, and like most things, you get what you pay for.

Everyone knows about Swiss Army knives. Understand that not all red plastic-handled knives are the genuine article. There are only two companies authorized to market "Swiss Army" knives. Victorinox and Wenger. Victorinox acquired Wenger in 2005 and they have decided to retain the Wenger nameplate. To determine the brand of a knife, open the blade. The brand is engraved on the ricasso (base of the blade). If it simply says "China" or "Pakistan" or "stainless" then keep looking, that is unless you're buying a cheap gift for your brother-in-law.

Some of the best quality knives are made right here in Oregon. Gerber, CRKT (Columbia River Knife and Tool), Benchmade, Kershaw and Leatherman, to name a few. These companies offer a wide selection of quality products. Most companies offer knives that appeal to the "survival" crowd. Once again, use wisdom when choosing a knife. Some so-called survival knives wouldn't help you survive a 30-second power outage much less a real emergency. Let me tell you about a couple of knives I own and recommend. First is a folding knife made by Tool Logic. It features one-handed opening, a built-in whistle, an LED flashlight and a magnesium fire striker. Cost is in the $50 range. The other is marketed by Bear Grylls of *Man vs. Wild* . Manufactured by Gerber, it is a fixed-blade knife. Incorporated into the design is a whistle, a firesteel, and a sharpening stone. The butt of the handle is designed to pound things like tent stakes, walnuts and even nails should the need arise. Cost is also in the $50 range. Neither are considered expensive but they were both gifts and they both have a built-in firesteel which makes them valuable as a survival tool.

Another must-have for your kit is a multi-tool. Multi-tools were made famous by Leatherman and have been copied by several other knife makers. All multi-tools have a knife blade, an assortment of screwdriver heads, a set of pliers and depending on the model, a saw, wire-cutter and mini-scissors. As most men already know, a good multi-tool is a valuable item to have.

Hunting Season

Southwestern Oregon has its fair share of hunters. We also have our fair share of deer and elk to keep the hunters coming back. Whether you cruise the back roads or hike the trails in search of your quarry, sooner or later you will run across someone who needs help. Some slide off into the ditch, others have a dead battery or some simply need directions, the trick lies in making sure it's the OTHER guy that gets in a pickle.

Some time back a hiker in Central Oregon got himself in trouble through a series of missteps. Hiking across the sagebrush-covered flats he somehow lost his water bottle. Seeing the river at the bottom of the canyon, he decided to hike down to get himself a drink. About halfway down he found himself in the proverbial pickle. He discovered he couldn't go down any farther but couldn't get back up either. He was on a ledge described as two feet by three feet in size. Conditions were such that rescuers were unable to reach him. After spending a chilly night on the ledge wearing jeans and a tank top, an Army National Guard Blackhawk helicopter plucked him from his predicament the next morning.

As it is with most 'pickles', the problem actually began hours before when he decided to take a hike. His choice of what to take and what to wear, coupled with his lack of good judgment added up to a precarious, life-threatening experience that didn't really have to happen.

His choice of clothing offered little in the way of protection from the chilly night air. Then he lost his water bottle. He had used his cell phone to call for help, but accidently dropped it during the course of the evening. A question I would ask is, "Was it all that important to get a drink?" Even if he made it to the river, that's not exactly potable water.

When hunters or hikers get in trouble, their situation can be greatly lessened with just a little planning. Cell phones are great and most of us carry one these days, but there are still a few hundred square miles in our region that have no coverage. Most of those square miles are where we like to play, hike, hunt, camp and otherwise recreate. Here are some suggestions. Pack like you're going to spend the night, even if you have no intent to do so. The kit I always carry in my pickup includes a jar of peanut butter, a couple of MREs, and some other snack food. Fire starting implements are a must and I also have a small tarp that could be fashioned into a shelter if the need arose. Then let someone know where you're going and what time you plan to return. These items, among others would go a long way toward keeping a person comfortable should you find yourself in that pickle.

Kids Prep

A few weeks back our electricity failed one evening in the midst of a wind storm. There were a couple of blinks and then total darkness. Flashlights in hand we fired up our Coleman lantern then settled down for an evening of "camping in". After a couple of hours of primitive living, my six year old grandson asked when the power was coming back on. I took some time to tell him about what might have happened to cause the outage and that right this minute there were crews out there working in the dark and the wind and rain to bring the electricity back. I assured him that by morning we would probably have our lights again. Sure enough, by the time we got up, electrical power was restored. There were no episodes of fear or overt insecurity, just frustration of trying to adjust to life without TV for the evening.

Children learn to take their cues from the adults in their lives. If the grownups are panicked, then children will likewise be undone. When the adults have made some simple preparations and are ready to handle the unexpected, it can serve well to bring stability and avoid all the drama associated with fears. Secondly, it is time well spent to explain what has happened, what is being done to fix things and how soon things might be expected to return to normal. You might ask if they are afraid. What are you afraid of? Reassure them that you

, and nothing bad is going to happen. ɹve plenty of food and supplies and ɟy are warm and well-fed and because ɹe and caring parent you have already prᴄ. ɹst such an emergency. No worries!

Dɪᴄ ɟ preparedness for kids can be a fun and exciting activity. Getting their own backpack and emergency gear can become a game. Picking out the perfect flashlight (don't forget extra batteries), gathering extra clothing and a spare toothbrush makes your kids feel like they're a part of the grand solution. The internet is loaded with resources for kids. FEMA has games, puzzles, cartoons and something called "Readiness U". Your children can even earn a certificate of graduation when they master Knowing the Facts, Making a Plan, Building a Kit, then they earn the right to graduate from Readiness U. This can all be found at www.ready.gov. How can you go wrong when you have help from Flat Stanley and Flat Stella to help your kids navigate their way to preparedness? Even NASA has a website designed especially for kids that offers tips on surviving hurricanes and other hazards.

So when you're making your plan and getting your kit together, involve the kids. They're always part of the plan anyway and they love to be involved in preparedness.

Making a List, Checking it Twice

Seems like most folks I talk with about disaster prep sooner or later ask for a list. At that point in the conversation I usually do one of two things. I tell them to just imagine not being able to go to the store for a long period of time. What would you need to get by? It's a little like planning a camping trip, what are you going to need? Make a list then lay in some supplies that would see you through most emergencies. The other option is to refer them to www.ready.gov or www.redcross.org. Both websites have excellent lists and suggestions for getting your kit together.

But for those who need that list right now, here's a good starter:

1. Water-at least a gallon per day per person.
2. Food-a three day supply of non-perishable food, (more is even better)
3. Radio-battery powered or hand-crank and a NOAA weather radio. Batteries for both
4. Flashlight and extra batteries (lots of batteries, and don't forget bulbs).
5. First aid kit.
6. Whistle-to signal for help
7. Moist towelettes, five gallon cans and garbage bags for sanitation purposes. (Eeeew) The term "bucket seat" takes on a whole new meaning.

The list can go on, but don't forget things like duct tape, zip ties, a wrench for shutting off the natural gas or propane, plastic sheeting, some cash, extra medications, and vitamins. This would be a good time to sit down with the family and brainstorm.

It is best to get a couple of totes and keep all your stuff in one place. Things like matches, candles, flashlights, batteries, some fuel canisters for your Coleman stove, and don't forget a hand-crank can opener. I know from experience that kits tend to 'grow' as you accumulate more essential items. Vitally essential items, you understand..

Your list is going to be different than your neighbor's. Their needs and priorities are different than yours. The needs of seniors will be different from the family that has an infant or children in the house. Also your home list is going to look differently than your "get home bag". That's the one you carry in your car to get you through an emergency if you happen to be away from home when disaster strikes.

If you're at a loss as to what to add to your list, there are dozens of websites that are eager to sell you a kit. Click your way to their site and go over the list of contents in their kits. You will get good ideas on what to put in your own kit.

I subscribe to the "Just Do Something!" school of thought. Even though you may be at a loss as to how to get started, just buying new batteries for your flashlight, maybe a few candles and some Spam (for the shelf, of course) is a move in the right direction.

Stress Management

Often following a tragic event, I note where those responsible for post-event management have brought in, not only food, shelter and medical care, but counselors to deal with confusion, survivors guilt or other mental distress. The most often heard phrase is, "remain calm." Remaining calm is NOT a natural response when your world has been shaken, your home burned or loved ones injured. Many times people feel the need to blame someone or something. This blame-placing urge usually results from a need to gain control of the situation by putting it into a familiar or understandable context. The usual targets for fixing blame are authority figures or government officials who should have done more to lessen the effects of the disaster.

Sometime back I had some friends who headed for a motel in a nearby town the minute their power went out. When I asked about using their camping gear to get by until the electricity was restored they acted like that had never occurred to them. It can be very unsettling when we find out how ill-prepared we are to handle a crisis.

It is important to be able to recognize and detect the signs of stress and/or shock during an emergency. Here are several warning signs that you may experience during emergency situations.

Physical signs: fatigue, upset stomach, shakiness, dizziness, heart palpitations, clamminess, disorientation, difficulty thinking, memory loss or loss of appetite.

Emotional signs: anxiety, grief, depression, irritability, feeling overwhelmed, thinking you or your loved ones will be harmed, nightmares or extreme fear.

When you are prepared, you are less likely to feel helpless and less likely to experience stress related disorders. You will remember what you discussed as a family and apply what you learned from those discussions and drills to help you overcome your situation.

Other things you can do now to help make a disaster less nerve-racking is to pack items in your emergency kits that you use in everyday life. For your children, pack coloring books, crayons, stories, gum, candy, stuffed animals and other useful items. For adults, pack a good book, a brush, razors, soap, playing cards, hard candy, paper and pen, medication, toilet paper and sundry items. These items can provide relief for stress during the times you have to wait for your life to return to normal.

Other stress-relieving items are desserts. Gelatin desserts, just-add-water, pudding, cake, muffin and cookie mixes, candy bars, popcorn, dehydrated fruits and fruit drinks. These items may seem frivolous, but they can really make a difference in helping you cope in an emergency.

Developing a positive attitude and learning coping and stress relieving methods will help you, not only in times of disaster, but throughout your life. So prepare now--it will be well worth the effort!

Supplies List

Last year, while Hurricane Isaac was reminding New Orleans residents why they should consider relocating, F.E.M.A. was reminding people how to stock up. Here's what F.E.M.A. says people should have on hand, in addition to a manual can opener and sufficient water supply:

Store at least a three day supply of non-perishable food. (I say more, but this is a good start.) Select foods that require no refrigeration, preparation or cooking and little or no water. Also choose items that are compact and lightweight. Avoid foods that will make you thirsty. Choose salt-free crackers, whole grain cereals, and canned foods with high liquid content.

- Ready-to-eat canned meats, fruits and vegetables
- Canned juices, milk, soup (if powdered, store extra water)
- Staples–sugar, salt, pepper
- High energy foods–peanut butter, jelly, crackers, granola bars, trail mix
- Vitamins
- Foods for infants, elderly persons or persons with special dietary needs
- Comfort/stress foods–cookies, hard candy, sweetened cereals, lollipops, instant coffee, tea bags

If your power goes out for more than a few hours, here are some recommendations for keeping your food safe as long as possible:

Keep the refrigerator and freezer doors closed as much as possible to maintain the cold temperature.

The refrigerator will keep food safely cold for about 4 hours if it is unopened. A full freezer will hold the temperature for approximately 48 hours (24 hours if it is half full) and the door remains closed.

Discard refrigerated perishable food such as meat, poultry, fish, soft cheeses, milk, eggs, leftovers and deli items after 4 hours without power.

Food may be safely refrozen if it still contains ice crystals or is at 40°F or below when checked with a food thermometer.

If the power has been out for several days, check the temperature of the freezer with an appliance thermometer. If the appliance thermometer reads 40°F or below, the food is safe to refreeze.

If a thermometer has not been kept in the freezer, check each package of food to determine its safety. If the food still contains ice crystals, the food is safe.

Undamaged, commercially prepared foods in all-metal cans and retort pouches (for example, flexible, shelf-stable juice or seafood pouches) can be saved.

Liberal doses of common sense are your best commodity, but staying informed, having your plan in place and getting your kit together can turn a potential disaster into "just another fire drill."

-Prescription medications. Check with your doctor and explain why you may need extras. Many doctors are sympathetic to the cause of disaster preparedness and are willing to prescribe extra meds. (Depending on the prescription.) The problem is your insurance company probably isn't quite so sympathetic so you can expect to pay for the extra pills out-of- pocket. Also don't forget to rotate your supplies as some medications lose their potency over time.

-Eyeglasses. Keeping an extra pair of glasses on hand is another example of good planning. Your optometrist will be happy to sell you an extra pair, but again, if you have vision coverage as a part of your health insurance plan, they usually offer very limited coverage anyway, so plan to pay for the additional cost out-of-pocket. I have noticed that some optical providers offer 2-for-1 deals from time to time so keep an "eye" out for those. (Sorry.)

-Pets and pet supplies. Don't forget your faithful companions when making preparations. If they are on some type of medication, ask your vet for additional supplies and explain why. I keep an extra sack of dog food on hand and continuously rotate it when needed.

For more suggestions, check out www.ready.gov and spend some time there. You will find lots of useful information.

If you haven't done so for a while, now would be a good time to give the starter rope on your generator a good pull. I gave mine a couple of dozen good pulls last week with no results. (Well I was worn out, but that's not exactly the result I was seeking!) After changing the spark plug, the gasoline and cleaning the carburetor, it now starts on the first pull. Ten minutes after the power goes out is not when you want to learn your standby generator is just going to keep on standing by. A spare spark plug, some Stabil (gasoline stabilizer) and a spare starter rope are inexpensive insurance for any small engine you may be relying on for an emergency.

Dave's 10 Foundational Principles of Disaster Preparedness

Call them core values, immutable truths or life rules, I feel one must develop their own personal "prepper philosophy" so there will be some direction and structure in your planning. Although mine are a work in progress, here they are:

1. Prepare BEFORE the disaster happens. I am always mildly amused and somewhat bewildered by the ones who run to the store either at the last minute or after the fact. That's a bit like having a fender bender then calling your insurance man to buy some coverage. In my observations of situations like Katrina and Sandy, I see people who had plenty of advance warning still getting caught empty-handed. The chaos, frustration and desperation that characterizes the unprepared can all be avoided by simply planning ahead. Your family is worth it. A biblical proverb says, "*A prudent person foresees danger and takes precautions. The simpleton goes on blindly and suffers the consequences.*" (Proverbs 22:3, New Living Translation) Plan ahead.

2. Avoid ready-made kits. There are literally thousands of ready-made kits available for purchase. Almost every disaster preparedness blog (except mine) has a kit for sale. I think some of them are pretty well thought out and actually very cool. However there is a

certain satisfaction in building your own, choosing quality components and actually designing the kit for your specific needs in your specific neighborhood. The person that lives miles out in the hills will have different needs than the person who lives right in town. Some families have babies and their kit will require diapers and anti-rash ointment. Others will have "seasoned citizens" in the household and their needs are unique to their circumstance. Check out the ready-mades to get ideas on what you might need, but make your own list, then fill it to your satisfaction.

3. Have a plan "B" and a plan "C." Every experienced battle commander knows his plan is perfect until the fighting begins. Most plans unravel somewhat once they're tested. This is a huge flaw I see in the National Geographic Channel's "Doomsday Preppers." Every featured group I have seen prepares for a specific disaster scenario. Just imagine how disappointed they'd be if they prepared for a nuclear attack and got hit with a coronal mass ejection (solar storm) instead. Now I am convinced if you live in hurricane country, then plan for a hurricane, but have two or more different evacuation routes. Prepare two or more retreat locations, just in case. If you live along the Oregon Coast, plan for an earthquake-tsunami episode, but always have a plan B. Your first escape route may be blocked with debris or a bridge may be impassable. Make alternate plans.

.

Being prepared is more than a full pantry of Spam, rice and beans. Preparedness begins with a mindset that says, "No matter what happens, we're going to get through any disaster thrown at us!" Accumulating extra stores and planning ahead is all part of the overall picture, but there should be some guiding principles behind how you prepare and for what reasons.

4. There is value in redundancy. An old joke among government employees is that somewhere deep in the bureaucracy swamp known as Washington, there is an agency known as the Department of Redundancy Department. This principle sounds a bit like #3, "Always Have a Plan B," but if you only have one way of purifying water, then two ways is even better. If you have one case of toilet paper, two is better. The more you have stored, the more you have available for barter or charity. Equally as important are the qualities of versatility and flexibility. Disasters don't follow a rigid design, so it's best if you design your plan with a certain adaptability factor as well.

5. Don't make preparations out of fear. Several months ago we held a class at our church on Disaster Preparedness. There were about 25 people in attendance. We discussed some of the reasons for prepping including the possibility of a mega-earthquake. After the class one of the attendees went home, gathered her children and pitched a tent out in the middle of a field in fear of an earthquake destroying her

house. I carry a spare tire in my car, not out of fear of a flat tire, but just in case. I have Band-aids in my wallet, just in case. The story is told of an 80 year old woman confronted by police. It was found she had two handguns in her purse, one in her glove box and a shotgun under the seat. The officer asked, "Ma'am, just what is it you are afraid of?"

Her reply, "Nothing!"

When you lay in extra stores, do so with the posture of "just in case." Not because you're afraid of what might happen.

6. Beware of "Style Over Substance!" Politicians are fond of making laws, usually with great pomp and volume that are long on publicity and short on actual effectiveness. We all know of products that don't live up to their billing. Not everything labeled "Survival" will be of benefit when actually put to the test. I am convinced that much so-called "survival" gear was designed by the P.T. Barnum School of Marketing. You'll recall their motto, I'm sure: "There's a sucker born every minute!" When making a purchase for your preparations, do your research and think it through. First ask yourself if you know how to use it. Then try to determine the probability of necessity if there is a disaster. Make smart, well informed purchases before you invest. It's not only your money at stake, your life may depend on this thing.

Principle #7. Develop useful skills. Learn to cook without relying on prepared, pre-packaged, "high in everything that's bad for you" fare. Practice getting by without a daily trip to the grocery store. Learn to fix things without calling a professional or buying new. I remember my dad building the most ingenious gate latches or other gizmo out of what he had on hand. The lessons learned in the Great Depression years stayed with him all his life. The "make do" philosophy has served our family well.

Principle #8. Get first aid training. Similar to #7 above, but so vital, it deserves its own category. Take a class in first aid. Build skills that will be invaluable if there are injuries in your neighborhood. Put together a first aid kit that includes such things as a suture kit, (available online), blood pressure cuff, and inflatable splints. There are video classes at www.redcross.com to teach skills in cardio-pulmonary resuscitation (CPR). Learn about triage and why hard decisions have to be made in times of disaster. When the time comes, you will be an asset rather than a liability. YouTube videos are a great source of information. For example if you need to learn to use that suture kit, there are YouTube videos covering the topic. Also check out the Patriot Nurse, a straight-talking prepper who pulls no punches when it comes to medical readiness.

Principle #9. Build relationships with your neighbors. Mapping Your Neighborhood is a program which gets you acquainted with your REAL first responders. When disasters strike, the Police, Fire and Emergency Medical Responders are all going to have their hands full with someone else's emergency. Having an inventory of your neighborhood skills is vitally important when it comes to response on a down home level. It is imperative you know who in your neighborhood may need your help and who has the skills to be of assistance. Are any of your neighbors elderly and may need assistance? How about propane tanks or natural gas shut-offs? All these questions are covered when neighbors get together and inventory their assets.

Principle #10. Spiritual preparedness. I may have saved the most important for last. Your core values and belief system will always be your first line of defense, and will be the first point of challenge in an emergency. How you are guided by your beliefs and values will dictate how well you respond and whether or not you will be successful. Time after time survivors interviewed after a disaster proclaim their strength to survive came from their faith.

Will you be a source of strength and stability for others or will you be yet another basket case demanding attention?

Disaster Preparedness
The Bible Version

Sometimes around our church, the topic of preparedness comes up in casual conversation. Among church folk, as in any other group, you will find a wide range of opinions. Some are die-hard preppers planning for the worst and others are mixing faith with foolishness and believe somehow they will be miraculously protected and provided for in the event of a disaster. Considering that, I researched the Bible and surprisingly I find there are quite a few references on the topic.

Beginning with the story of Joseph in Genesis (the coat-of-many-colors guy), it seems King Pharoah had a puzzling dream. The dream was about seven fat cows and seven skinny cows with the skinny cows eating up the fat cows. Joseph interpreted the dream to mean that there would be seven years of agricultural and economic plenty followed by seven years of famine. The overall message was to stock up during the good years so there would be no shortage when hard times came. (Genesis 41) Sure enough, Joseph advised Pharoah to stock up and when hard times came, there was plenty, not only for their own country, but enough to share. But it was only because they had heeded the warning and lay in supplies ahead of time.

Then there is the Proverb I have posted on my blog that says, "A prudent person foresees danger and takes precautions. The simpleton goes blindly on and suffers the consequences." Proverbs 22:3 (New Living Translation) The message there is that a fool gets warned and does nothing, while the wise person makes preparation against dangers.

Consider now the story of the ten virgins in the New Testament. (Matthew 25) They were waiting for a wedding. Half were ready, half were not. They are described as "five were wise, five were foolish." The five "preppers" were allowed access to the wedding and the other five were excluded. Although there are several interpretations of that story, I'm sure there's a lesson on preparedness in there somewhere. If failure to prepare equates to foolishness, then it would be wise to be ready.

And finally, Jesus held a powwow with the disciples the night he was arrested. (Luke 22) In essence He said, "Remember when I sent you out the last time, I told you not to take any money or supplies?" They all nodded in agreement. He continued, "Now this time when you go, make sure to take your knapsack, your money and some supplies. And also take a sword, if you don't have one, sell your coat and buy one." It doesn't take a master theologian to interpret or explain.

Great Resources

When I began writing on the topic, Disaster Preparedness was virtually looked upon as akin to joining a cult. "You believe what?" "You're doing what?" "That's a little weird!" Those are all comments that preppers hear from their non-prepping friends. In the past couple of years, Disaster Preparedness has gained some respectability with the help from National Geographic's "Doomsday Preppers" and a couple of dozen articles in the local media regarding the earthquake danger in our region. While I'm not exactly in full agreement with the case studies on "Doomsday Preppers" there are some things to be learned from them. In my opinion most of the groups depicted on there have settled on a favorite disaster scenario and focused totally on that particular perceived threat. You can get good ideas from their plan-making and incorporate their experience into your own preparations. I can't imagine the disappointment of the group who gets hit with a hurricane and all their planning has been how they're going to survive a nuclear holocaust. That may be just a tad bit facetious, but you get the hint. I believe that you should prepare for natural disasters that are common in your area. For example, here on the Oregon Coast, we rarely see tornados, so it would be foolish to build an underground "safe" room to go to in case of tornado. Rather the threats here are of high wind storms, (and the ensuing power outages) local flooding,(and the accompanying road closures) and of course earthquake.

Some have decided there will be a collapse of society through the demise of our economic system, political structure or a worldwide meltdown of both. Those folks tend to be a bit more hard-core than simply storing up a couple cases of Spam and some Ramen noodles.

If preparing for a disaster interests you, I have collected some websites that could be of value. Surprisingly one of the best sites is www.ready.gov. This site is sponsored by FEMA and is continually updated with accurate and valuable information. This site has links for individuals, businesses and even an area for kids. Included in the kids' section are some resources for teachers and parents. Another is www.redcross.org. The focus of The American Red Cross has always been emergency relief, but one of their primary missions is to provide training for anyone wants to improve their skills in First Aid, Caregiving and even Life Guarding. They even provide services for people who are displaced in disasters so they can re-connect with loved ones.

Our own Coos County Emergency Management is a division of the Coos County Sheriff's Office. Their website is well-designed and very informative. My favorite part is the "Are You Ready" booklet. This little booklet can be downloaded and assembled for your own reference. The best part of the booklet is the week-by-week Disaster Supply Llist that, if followed, will take you from Zero to well prepared in a six-month period.

The best time to prepare is before disaster strikes. That time is NOW!

Go Camping

One of the more popular summer activities in our area is always camping. We live in the middle of one of the most beautiful outdoor recreation areas in the world. No matter where you live in the South Coast region of Oregon, you are only a short drive from an amazing camping location. Whether you need full hookups for your home on wheels or simply a flat spot to pitch your tent, Southwestern Oregon has a camping experience to meet your need.

While I have always loved to go camping, not everyone is in love with a back-to-nature weekend. "Why would you want to pretend you're homeless?" "We have a nice house, why go live in a tent with no shower, no toilet and rough it?" It is a lot of extra work, and when you get home, you have to clean up your stuff and put it away while you're feeling grimy, tired and a little weird from eating too much junk food! On the "plus" side, you have just made an amazing memory with your kids!

But with all this being true, a family camping trip is a great way to test your disaster preparedness skills. How organized are you? I don't think I have ever gone camping when I didn't forget something I needed. A few years back I took my grandson up in the Siskiyou National Forest for a three-day trip. When we arrived at the Forest Service campground we set up the tent, arranged our ice chest full of food and it was then I discovered I had forgotten the Coleman stove. I took stock of my situation and decided to go it without the stove. It was too far to go back home and retrieve the thing, it was also too far to go to town and buy another one. Besides I looked at my menu and decided I could cook everything on my list over an open campfire. So we did. It wasn't as handy as the stove would have been, but other than blackening some of my cooking utensils, we made do with no serious consequences.

Maybe a camping trip would be a good shake-down cruise for your disaster preps. Make a list, check off the items and spend a weekend in the wild. You will invariably learn what you should have brought along. You will even learn what you could have left behind. If the power grid fails, or a major earthquake strikes, your camping gear will be your key to maintaining some kind of normalcy. If you have it arranged in a general location, you'll be able to lay your hands on what you need quickly. Maybe even in the dark. Your lantern, your cook stove, and other gear will get you through while your neighbors are still trying to hunt up their flashlight. While we're on the topic of your neighbors; once your home is stabilized, make sure your neighbors are ok. It's possible they are completely unprepared and are sitting in the dark hoping the lights come back on soon.

Normalcy Bias

Time to introduce a term that relates directly to disaster preparedness. Normalcy bias. Before I go any farther, I offer a disclaimer: I am not a psychologist, although I have been known to try (as an amateur) to get inside someone's head from time to time. I'm totally unqualified to comment on, analyze or otherwise complain about anyone's behavior. However, as we all know, that has never stopped any of us.

Normalcy bias is defined as the state of mind people enter when faced with a disaster. It causes people to underestimate both the possibility of a disaster occurring and its possible effects. This often results in situations where people fail to adequately prepare for a disaster, and on a larger scale, the failure of governments to include the populace in its disaster preparations. The assumption that is made in the case of the normalcy bias is that since a disaster never has occurred, then it never will.

Normalcy bias refers to our natural reactions when facing a crisis, that since something like this has never happened to me before, then it never will. It is human nature. Having a strong normalcy bias will prevent someone from preparing or planning for a disaster. Think ostrich-like behavior. Like a teenager with a fresh drivers license. He has never had an accident, so therefore it won't happen to him.

The normalcy bias often results in unnecessary deaths in disaster situations. When Hurricane Katrina hit New Orleans a few years ago, the government, at all levels, waited far too long to respond. Even as it became clear that the levee system was not going to work, tens of thousands of people stayed in their homes, directly in the line of the oncoming waves of water. People had never seen things get this bad before... so they simply didn't believe it could happen. As a result, nearly 2,000 residents died. The lack of preparation for disasters often leads to inadequate shelter, supplies, and evacuation plans. Even when all these things are in place, individuals with a normalcy bias often refuse to leave their homes. Studies show that more than 70% of people check with others before deciding to evacuate.

As Barton Biggs reports in his book, Wealth, War, and Wisdom: "By the end of 1935, 100,000 Jews had left Germany, but 450,000 still remained. Wealthy Jewish families kept thinking and hoping the worst was over." This may be one of the most tragic examples of the devastating effects of the "normalcy bias" the world has ever seen.

Perhaps the very first survival skill one could have is eliminating your normalcy bias. The realization that your comfort zone can change, and change quickly, is the first step towards being adaptable. It is impossible to think about or plan for disaster if your mind cannot accept that it could actually happen.

Planning to Live

When I first started making preparations I was convinced it was all about adding another can of Spam or some more beans to the pantry. The more I learn and the farther down this road I go, the more my thinking has evolved. Your plan is every bit as important as having your shelves full of food. You may have the most well-equipped pantry and every one of your cars has a get-home bag, but without a plan it may all be for naught.

Your response to disaster will be different if an earthquake occurs when you're 100 miles from home than it will be if you're sitting in your living room. When a fireman knocks on your door and says you have one hour to evacuate because of a wildfire heading your way, your plan has to be flexible enough to accommodate that scenario.

Some years back, as a student pilot, my flight instructor drilled into me the importance of always keeping a landing area in mind. There aren't too many flat areas in Western Oregon to land a small plane, but if I expected to survive an engine failure or other emergency, I'd better have a plan where I was going to land that airplane.

No plan can cover every scenario, but a primary basic to every disaster plan is communications. How do you plan to get in touch with your family? Have you discussed with your family who they should contact if they can't get in touch with you? One method widely encouraged by experts is to establish an out-of-state friend or relative to be a clearing-house for your family's communication. Many times it's easier to make an out of state call than to call next door. If local communications are disrupted, quite often calls out of the area are more successful than local calls.

So sit down with your family and decide which out of state relative or friend will make a good contact hub for you. Make sure each family member is supplied the necessary contact information and under which circumstances you will make contact.

Making plans isn't as exciting as finding a bargain on freeze-dried food or discovering another new gadget. But if you don't have a plan in place, none of the survival food nor the latest GPS receiver is going to be of any use to you. After all you've got to have a place picked out to land that airplane. Every pilot knows if they fly long enough, sooner or later they may have to make an emergency landing. You'd better have a plan! Remember the credo: Get a kit, make a plan, be informed! Don't overlook the 'plan' part.

Now Where Did I Put That?

We go to a lot of effort to gather our disaster kit. And now that we have it all together, ready for any emergency, where do we store it? Ideally we'd all have a storage pod that's burglar, fire and earthquake-proof. Situated somewhere handy, secure, temperature controlled, but out of the way, yet portable enough to load and move on a moment's notice.

I mentioned a while back that during an emergency, we sometimes don't think as clearly as when nobody is screaming. If your house is on fire, it's best to have a pre-arranged meeting place and alternate routes to get out of the house. If this is all decided ahead of time, then when the need arises, people won't need to be told what to do. My point is if your kit is scattered throughout the house, then you'll have to stop and think about where you've put all your stuff. For that reason it's best to keep it all in one place. Trying to round up your emergency gear in the middle of chaos is just that, chaos. I recommend you start with a couple of big totes then find a place for them. Which brings us to the next question. Where? In the basement? The attic? The storage shed?

Those choices may all be correct depending on your personal circumstances. Or not, depending on circumstances. In the event of an earthquake, it might not be a good idea to store your kit in the basement.

Some items, mostly foodstuffs, recommend storage in a cool, dry environment.

One person I know bought a surplus military communications "cube". It is six feet square, designed to house military radio gear and to be hauled in the back of a pickup. He remodeled the inside to organize his kit. It is weather tight and portable.

If you own an RV, you already have your cooking apparatus, probably some pots and pans and other supplies. In the event you'd need to evacuate you wouldn't have to round up all your gear. It's already in one place.

For the rest of us we need to find the best possible place that would keep our gear safe and accessible. It is impossible to plan for every contingency, but every home has a 'best' spot for storing your kit. Make it a family project, get some suggestions, do some brainstorming and I'll bet you can come up with the best location in your home to store your supplies.

Tech Ready

I have already confessed to being fascinated with gadgets. I'm pretty sure I'm in the majority. Otherwise how do you explain the millions of iPads out there and why is it the owner's manual for your smartphone now comes on a CD? Things are getting more and more complicated because that's what the public demands.

F.E.M.A (Federal Emergency Management Agency) has instituted a program titled "Get Tech Ready". This site is designed specifically for those who have grown accustomed to using technology as a matter of routine. My generation had to learn to come up to speed with computers. I remember taking a computer class with my wife in 1982 or 1983. The class was taught by a local high school teacher. The computers were Apple II's, as I recall. (Look that one up in the history books kids.) We came away from the class with the opinion that they could help keep the checkbook straight (maybe) and play some cool games, but that we would probably never have need for one in our home. (No wonder I could never make any money in the stock market!)

Get Tech Ready is a resource that educates families about how using technology can help them prepare for and recover from disasters. A survey by the American Red Cross shows that the internet, including news sites and social networking platforms is one of the most-used tools that people employ to let loved ones know they are safe.

Some preparedness tips offered by Get Tech Ready include: (1) Learn to use your mobile phone for alternative communication methods, such as texting and email, in the event voice communications are not available. (2) Store your personal and financial documents using a cloud-based (online) site or on a flash drive you always have handy. (3) Create an Emergency Information Document using the Ready.gov Family Emergency Plan template in Google Docs or by downloading the Ready FamilyEmergencyPlan to record your plans.

The American Red Cross has developed some very cool applications (apps) for your smartphone. They have a shelter finder app and another titled "Safe and Well", an amazing tool to let your loved ones know that you are indeed safe and well. It will also give you information regarding the whereabouts of your friends and family. It's time to shed your bias against technology and let technology work for you. It could, after all, keep your family alive. Computers, like the horseless carriage, television and rap music, are not going away.

Finally don't feel left out if you don't own a computer or don't know anything about today's seemingly complicated technology. It's never too late to learn and it might even be fun. Ask your grandkid to help you. After all I learned to text so I could stay in touch with my grandkids. You can do the same.

With the ongoing popularity of smartphones, it only makes sense to download one or more applications (apps) that will enhance your phone's usefulness in the event of a disaster. Most of today's smartphones come equipped with GPS capability that can link with other apps. For example I have an app on my phone called iTriage. This app was designed by a team of Emergency Room doctors. It will help in all kinds of on-the-spot emergency medical needs including a listing of nearby medical facilities. When choosing a hospital or trauma center, the GPS will then guide you to medical help. I realize that sounds like a bit of overkill, unless I'm visiting San Francisco and don't know my way around, then it suddenly becomes very valuable. All that from a free app. (All the apps mentioned in this column are free.)

Another is simply called "First Aid." It was developed by The American Red Cross and puts expert advice in your hands. This app is available for both iPhone and Android devices and allows instant access to the information you need to handle the most common first aid emergencies. It includes videos, interactive quizzes and simple step-by-step advice.

Yet another app from the Red Cross is titled "Earthquake". This one leads you through steps of preparation for the big one. Among the many features it sends you automatic notifications when there is a quake along with a directory for shelters in your local area. Another handy feature is that it allows you to send an "I'm safe" message to a pre-selected on-line site such as Facebook, Twitter, email or text message. Instructions and tips for building a survival kit are also included.

Other available applications include weather forecasting (The Weather Channel) ocean and surf advisories (NOAA), and river flood forecasting (also NOAA). There are some apps that provide tide information. Believe it or not, there are some instances in our area when high flood waters block the road, then when the tide goes out, the roads are briefly passable. Good information to have if you need to make that grocery run and are blocked by high water.

Every day it seems there are new applications available . If you shop around, or have an area of particular interest, there is a free app to meet your need. Learn to use the technology we have available to make your disaster preparations fun and productive.

Water

The Red Cross (www.redcross.org) and FEMA (www.ready.gov) are two of the best disaster preparedness online resources. Both websites urge the public to "Get a kit, make a plan, and be informed." The first item mentioned on both websites, under "get a kit" is water. Both organizations recommend storing a gallon per day per person for a three day period. Let me see, there are five people living at my house, three times five times three comes to... a lot of water. In fact the Red Cross says that the three day supply is only in the event you have to evacuate. For home purposes, you should have a two week supply on hand.

In reality, we can go several days without food, but water is essential to our existence. Without water we don't last very long. Clean, pure drinking water is a must. We seem to have an abundance of water in our area most of the year. However I can recall in recent history that both Powers and Coquille have issued "boil your drinking water" orders to their city water consumers. Even this past summer in Myrtle Point many of us stopped drinking city water because of an objectionable odor.

There are two primary ways to purify water: boiling and adding bleach. If tap water is unsafe because of water contamination (from floods, streams or lakes), boiling is the best method. Cloudy water should be

or adding bleach. Filter your water
, paper towels, cheese cloth or a
,nel.

э safest way to purify water. Bring the
ν   ,g boil for one minute then let the water
cool ᴗ   ᴨking.

If boᵢₗ ᴊ is not possible, treat the water by adding liquid household bleach, such as Clorox or Purex. Household bleach is typically between 5 percent and 6 percent chlorine. Avoid using bleaches that contain perfumes, dyes and other additives. Be sure to read the label.

Place the water (filtered, if necessary) in a clean container. Use basically ⅛ teaspoon of bleach per gallon of water up to ¼ teaspoon if cloudy or very cold. Mix thoroughly and allow to stand for at least 30 minutes before using (60 minutes if the water is cloudy or very cold). More information is available on the State of Washington, Department of Health website.

Personally I own a Big Berkey water filter that requires no electricity. It works with a ceramic filter system and strains out all the harmful bacteria. It even filters out objectionable odors as I found out this summer. Another option is one developed by the Texas Baptist Men's Water Ministry, who take their filter into areas recovering from a disaster. Check it out at www.monolithic.com. It is built from two five gallon plastic buckets with ceramic filters. You can even make your own. Buy the components and drill the appropriate holes in the buckets and bingo, instant water filter. I highly recommend that every home have a filter of some type to purify drinking water. Even if for no other reason than it smells nasty.

I have already confessed to being a gadget lover. Some gadgets are just that, gadgets. But I have just acquired a new "essential item" that you may want to add to your kit. I still get requests regarding storing sufficient quantities of water. I don't need to tell you of the necessity of having enough water on hand. I can also tell you that logistically speaking, it is usually not very practical to store that much water in your closet. The Red Cross (www.redcross.org) and FEMA (www.ready.gov) suggest that you make storing water a priority. The amounts seem to be a bit of overkill until you actually have to dip into your supply. If you are reduced to gathering rainwater off your roof or dipping water from a creek, then it must be purified. Boiling or adding bleach will do the trick. Boiling is considered the best method. Bring the water to a rolling boil for one minute then allow to cool. Unscented household bleach is typically between 5 and 6 percent chlorine. Cloudy water should be filtered before boiling or "bleached". Use ⅛ teaspoon of bleach per gallon of water and up to ¼ teaspoon if the water is cloudy or very cold.

I have noticed that several folks who depend on rain water, wells or springs, use an in-line, ultra-violet filter for purifying their household water. I won't try to go into the technical description of how UV rays work, but they have been in use for purifying water for nearly 100 years. Ultraviolet filters are simple and effective, capable of killing 99.99% of germs, parasites and other illness-causing organisms.

Now for the gadget. This item is called a steriPEN. It is about the same size and shape as a regular screwdriver. There are batteries in the handle and the "blade" portion of the thing is actually an ultra-violet wand. The one I have came with a water bottle and a built-in filter for use on cloudy water. Fill a container with water, then simply insert the wand portion into the water, push the button on the handle and use a stirring motion while you wait. In less than a minute, the green light comes on, indicating your water is now safe to drink. Watertight seals keep moisture away from the electronics. The company claims to be able to purify 16 oz of water in approximately 48 seconds, while a 32 oz. container takes roughly 90 seconds. Cost varies from $50.00 up to the $200.00 range, depending on the model you choose. When's the last time you visited a foreign country and felt comfortable drinking their water? Has your municipality issued a "boil your water" order lately? This item would be handy for any foreign travel and also whenever you had a question about your water.

I carry mine in my get home bag in the event something happens and I have to spend unexpected time away from home. Check it out and see if this is something in which you might want to invest.

During a major disaster, water mains may break, the municipal water processing system may fail or plumbing may be disrupted. Something we take for granted, a flushing toilet may not be available. In the event of an earthquake, it's not too much of a stretch to expect that your plumbing, both incoming and outgoing could be disrupted.

Human waste, if not disposed of properly, can not only cause a sanitation and hygiene mess but if not managed properly will spread disease.

For those who live in rural areas and your water source is a spring, you may be in good shape, barring any damage to your plumbing. Our disaster preparedness plan isn't complete until we have considered some alternative way to dispose of waste.

Several solutions are available from a toilet seat that snaps to the top of a five-gallon bucket for $10, to a chemical porta-potty costing $200 plus. If you opt for the five-gallon bucket solution, don't forget to get some small trash bags to use as liners.

The 2010 earthquake in Haiti taught responders several lessons. In a region that was marginally sanitary in the best of times, it became painfully aware that in a post-event environment, the health climate deteriorated rapidly and drastically because of the lack of adequate sewage capability. Health officials are still battling a cholera epidemic in Haiti since their earthquake. Any disruption of sanitary service poses significant health risks. Every so often a major city experiences a shutdown of garbage services. The mountains of accumulated trash are an attractive nuisance to all sorts of disease-bearing vermin, including rats, mice and dog packs.

On a different note, researchers are learning about compost piles and their drawbacks after a disaster. Composting is basically managing the decomposition of certain biodegradable products. In other words and in base terms: it is simply a managed collection of garbage intended for a noble purpose, eventually. (My apologies to all organic gardeners everywhere.) The word of caution here is to insure that your compost pile is well-secured and does not get scattered nor become an attractant for disease-bearing rodents or other scavengers. Communities will have their hands full with trying to restore basic services without worrying about the runaway rat population.

Kit Building

Lets revisit the motto: Get a kit, make a plan, be informed. I get comments nearly every day about this column. Most everyone is positive and say they enjoy the information. When I ask whether or not they're actually doing the stuff, quite often they admit that they know they should, but just haven't gotten started yet. Both F.E.M.A and the Red Cross recommend having a 72 hour emergency kit. That is having enough supplies and equipment to get you through three days without electricity, water or trips to the store. Just for the record I think 72 hours is a good start, but a 14 day kit is even better. Maybe we should ask the folks back east if they think 72 hours is enough.

One of the concerns I often hear is, "I'm just not sure where to begin." So here is a step-by-step, seven week kit-building plan. At the end of seven weeks, if you follow the steps, you will have a kit that will get you through the first 72 hours of most disasters. Not only will you will have a kit, but you will have a plan in place that will increase your family's chances of survival. Keep in mind it is my experience that kits naturally grow because once you begin you keep finding essentials that you just can't live without. So let's get started.

Things to purchase Week 1:

1. A battery-powered radio, one with a N.O.A.A. weather channel and extra batteries.
2. Flashlights or battery powered lanterns (with extra batteries, of course) Avoid using candles because of the fire hazard.
3. Water to last three days. At least one gallon per person per day. Start with one gallon this week.

Tips for Week 1:

1. Start with these items that emergency responders consider the most critical to getting you through the first 72 hours until basic services may be restored.
2. Don't be overwhelmed by a huge list of items. I've identified the most important things. Just buy a few items each week for seven weeks and you will be prepared for the most likely emergencies in our area.
3. Commercially bottled water is recommended to ensure safety. Replace before "use by" date expires.

I suggest you keep your kit in one general location. That way, when the power is out, you won't be running around in the dark searching for your stuff. Every household is different and each house has a 'best,' if not ideal spot for your emergency kit. If you have a container in which to store your gear, all the better. One friend of mine uses an old ice chest for certain essentials. But most any good quality "tote" will suffice.

Building Your Kit
Week 2

Week Two shopping list:

1. Manual can opener.
2. First aid kit. Should start with gauze and bandages, tweezers, scissors and antiseptic ointment. Add some hydrogen peroxide, alcohol, suture kit, the list is endless.
3. Airtight bags, storage containers and a permanent marker. I find that both two gallon and five gallon buckets with lids are ideal for storage. Use the marker to list the contents and the date.
4. Extra prescription medications, eyeglasses and contact lens solutions. Collaborate with your doctor on this one. He (or she) will probably be sympathetic once you explain why you need extras. Your insurance provider may not be as sympathetic, but you might work with your pharmacy on this one.
5. Bring home another gallon of water.

6. Non-perishable food. Start with a few cans of meat, fruits, some peanut butter and crackers. Try to stick with food that you are accustomed to eating.
7. Plastic sheeting, tarp and duct tape.

Tips for Week Two:

1. Collect your supplies in one place. When the lights are out and confusion reigns, it is just simpler when your kit is together.
2. Consider having two kits. One at home and one in your car. Not everyone is at home when disaster strikes. There is a multitude of kits on the market, but it is still best to build your own.
3. Rotate your stock of food, water, medicines and batteries every six months to ensure freshness.

Building Your Kit
Week 3

Things to buy for Week Three:

1. Dust filter masks. Look for the ones rated "N95", they are designed to keep out airborne dust, pollen and possibly protection from disease.
2. Whistle to signal for help.

3. Finish buying water, at least one gallon per person per day.
4. Cash. Set aside as much as you can reasonably afford. Small bills are best. During a widespread power outage your debit card is of no value. Neither is the money you have stashed in a savings account.
5. Make copies of your important family documents. You can scan them to a flash drive and store in either a "go bag" or other safe location away from your home. These documents may include copies of insurance policies, deeds, passports, birth certificates and titles to your vehicles.
6. Regular, unscented, household bleach for purifying water. Also pick up an eyedropper. Experts recommend 16 drops of bleach to purify one gallon of water.
7. Juice. Get the single-servings as refrigeration may not be available
8. Nutrition/high energy bars

Tips:

Plan and discuss how you would evacuate your home in the event of a sudden emergency.

Tap water may need to be purified with bleach in the event of a disaster. Consider purchasing or building a stand-alone water filter. (Email me for a free set of plans to build a filter.)

Plan to have at least one can of meat or meat entree for each family member per day.

Select two places to meet with your family after an emergency or disaster-one near your home and one outside of your neighborhood in case it's not safe to return.

Building Your Kit
Week 4

Things to buy Week Four:

1. Disposable camera with flash for documenting damage. While I'm on the topic of photographic documentation, now would be a good time to get a video inventory of your home and its contents. If you have a video camera, simply walk through your house and give a running commentary on your possessions, value and when purchased. Invaluable

2. Utility knife and/or scissors. This is separate from the scissors in your first-aid kit. These are for heavy-duty cutting. Hundreds of uses for sharp cutting instruments.

3. Heavy duty trash bags

4. Matches in waterproof container. Be sure to get the "strike anywhere" style. Matches are like duct tape and zip-ties, you can never have too many.
5. Sanitizing wipes. Good for cleaning things other than the baby's bottom; like your hands, face and elsewhere!
6. Extra set of car and house keys. Store them in a secure location away from your primary residence.
7. Fruit, canned or snack-pack.

Tips:

Begin thinking about packing a "go bag" with a condensed version of your home emergency kit in case you need to relocate temporarily.

Stay in the habit of keeping your gas tank half full and keeping your cell phone charged.

If you need to evacuate, be sure to remember your car phone charger. Better yet, get an extra and carry it in your glove box.

Building Your Kit
Week 5

Shopping list for Week Five:

1. Gloves. Latex or non/latex, plus a good pair of work gloves.
2. Paper plates, cups and utensils
3. Canned vegetables, soup/stew.
4. Toilet paper (lots) and paper towels.
5. Travel sizes of personal hygiene items, dental care, soap, feminine care, deodorant, etc.
6. Disinfectant wipes.
7. Supplies for baby, elderly or special needs.

Tips for Week Five

Select an emergency contact person residing out of the area for family members to contact in case they are separated. Sometimes it's easier to connect a phone call out of the area than it is locally.

Keep a copy of this seven week list in your car when you go shopping. Check off items as you go.

Make sure that all adults and teens in your household know how to shut off water and utilities.

Never use a portable generator in an enclosed area. Follow the manufacturer's instructions.

Building Your Kit
Week 6

Things to buy for Week Six:

1. Blankets and small pillows. A good quality sleeping bag is a good substitute.
2. Towels. Set aside some extra towels and if you are preparing a go-bag for each family member, a towel is a must-have.
3. Extra clothing and outerwear, and sturdy, comfortable footwear.
4. Small photo album with current photos of family members and pets
5. Assorted crackers and nuts (low salt or salt-free are best to reduce thirst).

Tips for Week Six:

Do you have home fire extinguishers? Are they rated ABC? If so check with your local fire department to have them inspected and when they should be replaced. Residential fires are the most frequent disasters and having a working fire extinguisher can mean the difference between minor damage and losing your home.

Consider using five gallon plastic buckets with lids for storing your supplies. They are light, strong, and dust, water and bug-proof, and relatively inexpensive. Remember to pick up a "lid lifter" at your hardware store. You can also ask the hardware store lady (or man) if they are "food grade" plastic. Markings on the bottom of the bucket tell the tale.

Mark your storage containers with a permanent marker. Also mark expiration dates and plan to rotate supplies every six months. Some folks use the change to Daylight Savings Time to remind them it's time to change out the old stuff for new.

Building Your Kit
Week 7

Week 7 Shopping List:

1. Small tool kit. Include a wrench (slip-joint wrench like "Channellocks" or water pump pliers) for shutting off utilities, hammer, nails, screwdrivers, screws, duct tape, zip ties and on and on and on...I This is one aspect of the kit that can grow, swell and improve with every trip to the hardware store.
2. Signal flares.
3. Insect repellent. While we're on this topic, I have recently read about people using wasp/hornet spray for personal defense. It's less expensive than pepper spray, reaches out at least 20 feet

and temporarily incapacitates anyone intent on causing you harm.

4. Sunscreen.
5. Granola or dry cereal.
6. Extra pet food. Also if your pet requires medication, get some extra for them as well. Also don't forget, your pet requires water.
7. Fire extinguisher. Be sure it carries the ABC rating. If you need training in its use, contact your local fire department.

Tips:

Be sure to include pets in your plan.

When you leave town, take your go-bag along. Disasters don't always happen while you're at home.

Keep your car's gas tank above ½ tank. You never know when you get that call in the middle of the night to go visit your ailing, wealthy aunt in the hospital. Not a time to be out of gas and none available.

As I have mentioned before survival is not a kit. Survival is a plan and the kit should be a part of your plan. It is best to keep your kit in a single location, not strewn about the house, some things in one closet, other items in the basement and yet other things stacked in the garage. Try to set aside an area for all your gear and supplies. When the power goes out and things are mildly chaotic at your house, you don't want to be searching in the dark for your stuff. Make sure the battery powered lantern is the most easily-located item in your inventory. The power seldom goes out during daylight hours. Flashlights, lanterns and other lighting devices are the first things you will want to get operational.

Funny thing about Disaster Preparedness, our parents and grandparents simply 'put up' their garden produce, butchered a half a beef and froze it and otherwise laid up stores for the winter months. The current generation goes to the store nearly every day to decide what to have for dinner, has no idea what to do with real flour and is nearly crippled without electricity.

With all the microwaveable conveniences and our fast-food on-demand mentality, the thought of actually preparing in case something goes wrong is often times a foreign concept.

Nevertheless, there are some of us who remember life without microwave ovens and Hamburger Helper. Some who have lived through events that knocked out power and weather which precluded safe travel. Improving conditions during times of difficulty can be as simple as having some extra food on hand, or a camping stove or alternative lighting or maybe just fresh batteries for the flashlight.

CPSIA information can be obtained
at www.ICGtesting.com
Printed in the USA
LVOW11s0254180917
549086LV00001B/1/P